DIVING LOG BOOK

aquapress

Copyright © 2005 AquaPress

The right of AquaPress to be identified as the author of this work has been asserted in accordance with the Copyright Designs and Patents Act, 1988.

All rights reserved

This book is sold subject to the condition that it shall not, by way of trade or otherwise, be lent, resold, hired out, or otherwise circulated without the publisher's prior consent in any form of binding or cover other than that in which it is published and without a similar condition including this condition being imposed on the subsequent purchaser.

An AquaPress Book

Published and distributed from AquaPress
25 Farriers Way
Temple Farm Industrial Estate
Southend-on-Sea
Essex, SS2 5RY
United Kingdom
www.aquapress.co.uk

First published 2005

A CIP catalogue record for this book is available from the British Library

All illustrations and photographs Copyright © AquaPress 2005

Diving is a potentially hazardous practice. This log book is intended as a source of information only and is not intended as a substitute for specialized training, equipment or experience. The publishers accept no responsibility for any loss, injury or inconvenience sustained by any person using this book.

For information on all other AquaPress titles including log books visit our website: www.aquapress.co.uk

ISBN: 1-9054920-1-4

Property of

Name

Address

Phone

In Emergency Contact:-
Name
Address

Phone _____ Mobile _____

Highest Diving Qualification

MEDICAL INFORMATION

Date of Birth
Blood Type
Allergies
Medication

Known
Disorders or
Conditions

Medical Certificate No.
Self Assessment Valid Until __/__/__ __/__/__ __/__/__ __/__/__

TRAVEL/DIVE INSURANCE

Company
Policy Number
Emergency Tel
Valid Until __/__/__ __/__/__ __/__/__ __/__/__

Welcome to the second edition of the AquaPress Diving Log Book.
This new edition is now even larger allowing you to log 100 dives and incorporates many updates making it even easier to keep an accurate record of your dives.
The changes allow more flexibility, and the new graph paper area allows space to record your dive profile, a map of the site or just simply continue writing your notes.

We hope you enjoy using your logbook however, if you have any comments or suggestions we'd love to hear from you. Simply write to the address given in the preface or contact www.aquapress.co.uk

Enjoy your diving

Notes to usage

This logbook is designed for recreational use only. If you are performing any work underwater or are being paid for diving please use a suitable commercial diving log book.

This logbook is aimed at recreational divers who are diving for the majority of the time on air. The logbook may be used for decompression dives and nitrox dives. For nitrox dives we recommend that a record is made of the mixture used and other operational limiting factors such as maximum operating depth for each dive.

Your dive log book contains all the information that is required to be recorded by law. In addition, there are many other areas of information that are included for information and reference. All the information required by the HSE (Health & Safety Executive) Recreational ACOP's (Approved Code of Practice) are highlighted with a bold outline. In addition to these requirements you should also record the breathing mixture used if using anything other than air; any episode of barotrauma, discomfort or injury suffered and details of any decompression illness and the treatment given; any emergency or incident of special note which occurred during the dive and any other factor relevant to your health and safety.

Each page is divided into distinct sections which should be completed and read from left to right and top to bottom. Completing the dive log in this manner will ensure that all vital information is recorded and information useful for future dives will be ready for reference. Of course the amount of information recorded for each dive will depend upon a number of factors. For example on a multi-day live-aboard there would be little use in entering the same information (which remains static) for each and every dive.

AIR

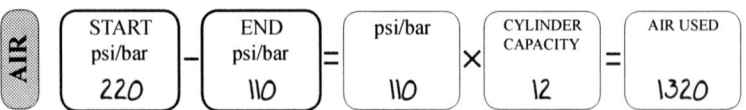

Completing the AIR column from left to right enables you to calculate easily the total amount of air used. It should be noted however, that skip breathing and other breath holding methods used while scuba diving are highly dangerous and on no account should you attempt to lower this figure by saving air. On the contrary this figure should be used as an indicator for advanced dive planning. The only acceptable way of reducing your air consumption should be through improved physical fitness.

TIME.

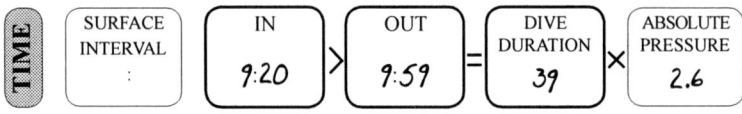

Many log books use a system of tick boxes for 1st Dive, 2nd Dive, 3rd Dive etc. If you do not have a surface interval recorded then the dive by default becomes your 1st dive of the day! Entering the time in/time out will allow you to calculate your dive duration. Alternatively this may be taken from your watch or dive computer. At the same time you may wish to complete part of the next table namely Maximum Depth.

SURFACE AIR BREATHING RATE

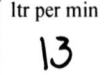

Because of the way the tables are positioned you will be able to calculate your surface air breathing rate with little effort. Record your Air Used (Cylinder Capacity x bar) then divide this by the result of your absolute pressure [Depth + 1 (Surface Atmospheric Pressure)] multiplied by your dive duration. This calculation gives your surface air breathing rate in litres per minute. This is an excellent indicator which may be compared across dives of varying nature and may be used to create highly accurate dive plans. A higher figure would indicate increased stress and workload for a particular dive.

DECO – DEPTH

DECOMPRESSION / SAFETY STOPS	PRE DIVE GROUP	MAX DEPTH	END DIVE GROUP
_3_ mins at _3_ m/ft _21_ %		16m	
____ mins at ____ m/ft ____ %			
____ mins at ____ m/ft ____ %	Safety Margin: None (5%) 10% 15% 20%		

Computer / Decompression Tables Used: **BSAC '88**

The type of training and tables you are using will depend on how you use this column. If you are completing No-Decompression dives then your tables may still advocate the use of a safety stop at a particular depth which may be recorded here. Depending on the type of tables you are using you may also wish to record your Pre Dive and End Dive Groups in the boxes provided. At the other end of the scale if you are conducting Accelerated Decompression Stops then you have the space to include up to three stops and the breathing mixture used.

It is important to record the type of computer or decompression table used. All computers and tables are not the same and do not provide the same times. For this same reason you may wish to think about (and record) what safety margin you are using. Do you always end your dive when your computer bleeps at you?

WEIGHT – EXPOSURE

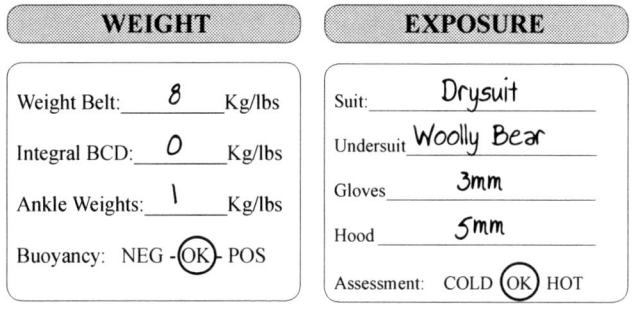

Recording your weight and exposure levels will help you to understand what works for you in a particular situation. Any adjustment necessary for example, to stop you from being too cold or too positively buoyant, can be made for your next dive.

DCI RISK

DCI RISK

Was this dive...
Cold Water Dive ☑
Decompression Dive ☐
Deep Dive ☐
Excessive Work ☐
Missed Deco. Stops ☐
Rapid Ascent ☐
Are you...
Dehydrated ☐

All the factors that are listed in this table are known to make a diver more susceptible to suffering from decompression illness. The more boxes that you tick for each dive the more conservative your dive should be. As a general indicator a cold water dive is in water less than 10°C and any dive greater than 30m should be regarded as a deep dive. A good if rather crude indicator as to whether you are dehydrated or not is to look at the colour of your urine before the dive. Some technical agencies are now incorporating this in their records in the following manner L M D – light, medium or dark colour. Ideally the colour should always be light. Dehydration is normally associated with tropical and warm water diving but we should remember that it can also be a contributing factor to decompression illness even in cold water dives.

TIDES

TIDES

HIGH WATER 07 : 19

LOW WATER 13 : 54

SLACK WATER 09 : 24

CURRENT _____ kn   DIRECTION _____ °

If you are diving in the sea then you are diving in a tidal environment, even if you are diving in a so called non-tidal area of the world where tides are in fact so small that they are disregarded. It is important therefore to know the time of slack water and when your window of opportunity for diving exists. If you are conducting a drift dive then it would be highly advisable to also determine the direction and speed of the tide.

SEA CONDITIONS

SEA CONDITIONS

SEA STATE CALM

WATER TEMP 15°C

VISIBILITY 3-4m

BEAUFORT SCALE 1

Of all the items listed probably the most subjective is visibility. Poor visibility in the Red Sea would normally be regarded as superb off the East Coast of England!

The Beaufort Scale devised back in 1805 by Rear-Admiral, Sir Francis Beaufort is a widely recognised tool for describing sea conditions:-

THE BEAUFORT SCALE

No.	Knots	Mph	Description	Effects at sea
0	0	0	Calm	Sea like a mirror
1	1-3	1-3	Light air	Ripples, but no foam crests
2	4-6	4-7	Light breeze	Small wavelets
3	7-10	8-12	Gentle breeze	Large wavelets crests, not breaking
4	11-16	13-18	Moderate wind	Numerous whitecaps
5	17-21	19-24	Fresh wind	Many whitecaps, some spray
6	22-27	25-31	Strong wind	Larger waves form. Whitecaps everywhere. More spray
7	28-33	32-38	Very strong wind	White foam from breaking waves begins to be blown in streaks
8	34-40	39-46	Gale	Edges of wave crests begin to break into spindrift
9	41-47	47-54	Severe gale	High waves. Sea begins to roll. Spray may reduce visibility
10	48-55	55-63	Storm	Very high waves with overhanging crests. Blowing foam gives sea a white appearance
11	56-63	64-72	Severe storm	Exceptionally high waves
12	63	73	Hurricane force	Air filled with foam. Sea completely white. Visibility greatly reduced

EQUIPMENT

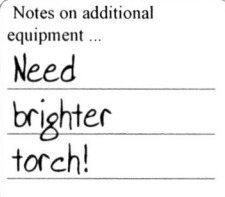

Space to record any additional information which is relevant to the particular dive.

DIVE PROFILE/DRAWING

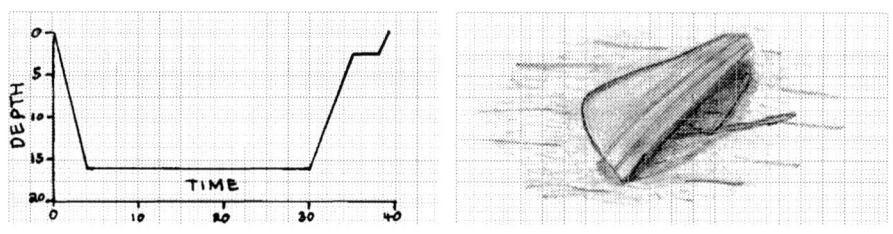

The graph paper at the bottom of the second page may be used to produce a dive profile or to record the details of a particular dive site.

Dive Record

Dive No **Date**

Dive Site

AIR: START psi/bar − END psi/bar = psi/bar × CYLINDER CAPACITY = AIR USED

SURFACE AIR BREATHING RATE = ____ ltr per min

TIME: SURFACE INTERVAL : | IN : > OUT : = DIVE DURATION × ABSOLUTE PRESSURE

DECO - DEPTH:
DECOMPRESSION / SAFETY STOPS
____ mins at ____ m/ft ____ %
____ mins at ____ m/ft ____ %
____ mins at ____ m/ft ____ %

PRE DIVE GROUP | MAX DEPTH | END DIVE GROUP

Safety Margin: None 5% 10% 15% 20%

Computer / Decompression Tables Used:

WEIGHT

Weight Belt: ____ Kg/lbs
Integral BCD: ____ Kg/lbs
Ankle Weights: ____ Kg/lbs
Buoyancy: NEG - OK - POS

EXPOSURE

Suit: ____
Undersuit ____
Gloves ____
Hood ____
Assessment: COLD OK HOT

DCI RISK

Was this dive...
Cold Water Dive ☐
Decompression Dive ☐
Deep Dive ☐
Excessive Work ☐
Missed Deco. Stops ☐
Rapid Ascent ☐
Are you...
Dehydrated ☐

TIDES

HIGH WATER :
LOW WATER :
SLACK WATER :
CURRENT ____ kn   DIRECTION ____ °

SEA CONDITIONS

SEA STATE
WATER TEMP
VISIBILITY
BEAUFORT SCALE

EQUIPMENT

Notes on additional equipment ...

Skipper **Boat**

Accumulated Dive Time To Date	Dive Time this Dive	Total Dive Time To Date
:	:	:

Verification Signature   Certification No.

Dive Record

Dive No | **Date**

Dive Site

AIR

START psi/bar − END psi/bar = psi/bar × CYLINDER CAPACITY = AIR USED

SURFACE AIR BREATHING RATE = ltr per min

TIME

SURFACE INTERVAL : | IN : > OUT : = DIVE DURATION × ABSOLUTE PRESSURE

DECO - DEPTH

DECOMPRESSION / SAFETY STOPS

____ mins at ____ m/ft ____ %

____ mins at ____ m/ft ____ %

____ mins at ____ m/ft ____ %

PRE DIVE GROUP | MAX DEPTH | END DIVE GROUP

Safety Margin: None 5% 10% 15% 20%

Computer / Decompression Tables Used:

WEIGHT

Weight Belt: _____ Kg/lbs

Integral BCD: _____ Kg/lbs

Ankle Weights: _____ Kg/lbs

Buoyancy: NEG - OK - POS

EXPOSURE

Suit: _____

Undersuit _____

Gloves _____

Hood _____

Assessment: COLD OK HOT

DCI RISK

Was this dive...
- Cold Water Dive ☐
- Decompression Dive ☐
- Deep Dive ☐
- Excessive Work ☐
- Missed Deco. Stops ☐
- Rapid Ascent ☐

Are you...
- Dehydrated ☐

TIDES

HIGH WATER :

LOW WATER :

SLACK WATER :

CURRENT _____ kn   DIRECTION _____ °

SEA CONDITIONS

SEA STATE

WATER TEMP

VISIBILITY

BEAUFORT SCALE

EQUIPMENT

Notes on additional equipment ...

_____

_____

_____

_____

Skipper | **Boat**

Accumulated Dive Time To Date	Dive Time this Dive	Total Dive Time To Date
:	:	:

Verification Signature Certification No.

Dive Record

Dive No | **Date**

Dive Site

AIR

START psi/bar − END psi/bar = psi/bar × CYLINDER CAPACITY = AIR USED

SURFACE AIR BREATHING RATE = ltr per min

TIME

SURFACE INTERVAL : | IN : > OUT : = DIVE DURATION × ABSOLUTE PRESSURE

DECO - DEPTH

DECOMPRESSION / SAFETY STOPS

_____ mins at _____ m/ft _____ %

_____ mins at _____ m/ft _____ %

_____ mins at _____ m/ft _____ %

PRE DIVE GROUP | MAX DEPTH | END DIVE GROUP

Safety Margin. None 5% 10% 15% 20%

Computer / Decompression Tables Used:

WEIGHT

Weight Belt: _____ Kg/lbs

Integral BCD: _____ Kg/lbs

Ankle Weights: _____ Kg/lbs

Buoyancy: NEG - OK - POS

EXPOSURE

Suit: _____

Undersuit _____

Gloves _____

Hood _____

Assessment: COLD OK HOT

DCI RISK

Was this dive...
Cold Water Dive ☐
Decompression Dive ☐
Deep Dive ☐
Excessive Work ☐
Missed Deco. Stops ☐
Rapid Ascent ☐
Are you...
Dehydrated ☐

TIDES

HIGH WATER :

LOW WATER :

SLACK WATER :

CURRENT _____ kn   DIRECTION _____ °

SEA CONDITIONS

SEA STATE

WATER TEMP

VISIBILITY

BEAUFORT SCALE

EQUIPMENT

Notes on additional equipment ...

Skipper | **Boat**

Accumulated Dive Time To Date	Dive Time this Dive	Total Dive Time To Date
:	:	:

Verification Signature **Certification No.**

Dive Record

Dive No	Date

Dive Site

AIR

START psi/bar − END psi/bar = psi/bar × CYLINDER CAPACITY = AIR USED

SURFACE AIR BREATHING RATE = ____ ltr per min

TIME

SURFACE INTERVAL :

IN : > OUT : = DIVE DURATION × ABSOLUTE PRESSURE

DECO - DEPTH

DECOMPRESSION / SAFETY STOPS

_____ mins at _____ m/ft _____ %

_____ mins at _____ m/ft _____ %

_____ mins at _____ m/ft _____ %

PRE DIVE GROUP

MAX DEPTH

END DIVE GROUP

Safety Margin: None 5% 10% 15% 20%

Computer / Decompression Tables Used:

WEIGHT

Weight Belt: _____ Kg/lbs

Integral BCD: _____ Kg/lbs

Ankle Weights: _____ Kg/lbs

Buoyancy: NEG - OK - POS

EXPOSURE

Suit: _____

Undersuit _____

Gloves _____

Hood _____

Assessment: COLD OK HOT

DCI RISK

Was this dive...
Cold Water Dive ☐
Decompression Dive ☐
Deep Dive ☐
Excessive Work ☐
Missed Deco. Stops ☐
Rapid Ascent ☐
Are you...
Dehydrated ☐

TIDES

HIGH WATER :

LOW WATER :

SLACK WATER :

CURRENT _____ kn   DIRECTION _____ °

SEA CONDITIONS

SEA STATE

WATER TEMP

VISIBILITY

BEAUFORT SCALE

EQUIPMENT

Notes on additional equipment ...

_____

_____

_____

_____

_____

Skipper   Boat

Accumulated Dive Time To Date	Dive Time this Dive	Total Dive Time To Date
:	:	:

Verification Signature   **Certification No.**

Dive Record

Dive No | **Date**

Dive Site

AIR

| START psi/bar | − | END psi/bar | = | psi/bar | × | CYLINDER CAPACITY | = | AIR USED |

SURFACE AIR BREATHING RATE = _____ ltr per min

TIME

| SURFACE INTERVAL : | | IN : | > | OUT : | = | DIVE DURATION | × | ABSOLUTE PRESSURE |

DECO - DEPTH

DECOMPRESSION / SAFETY STOPS

_____ mins at _____ m/ft _____ %
_____ mins at _____ m/ft _____ %
_____ mins at _____ m/ft _____ %

PRE DIVE GROUP | MAX DEPTH | END DIVE GROUP

Safety Margin: None 5% 10% 15% 20%

Computer / Decompression Tables Used:

WEIGHT

Weight Belt: _____ Kg/lbs

Integral BCD: _____ Kg/lbs

Ankle Weights: _____ Kg/lbs

Buoyancy: NEG - OK - POS

EXPOSURE

Suit: _____
Undersuit _____
Gloves _____
Hood _____
Assessment: COLD OK HOT

DCI RISK

Was this dive...
Cold Water Dive ☐
Decompression Dive ☐
Deep Dive ☐
Excessive Work ☐
Missed Deco. Stops ☐
Rapid Ascent ☐
Are you...
Dehydrated ☐

TIDES

HIGH WATER :

LOW WATER :

SLACK WATER :

CURRENT _____ kn   DIRECTION _____ °

SEA CONDITIONS

SEA STATE

WATER TEMP

VISIBILITY

BEAUFORT SCALE

EQUIPMENT

Notes on additional equipment ...

Skipper | **Boat**

Accumulated Dive Time To Date	Dive Time this Dive	Total Dive Time To Date
:	:	:

Verification Signature Certification No.

Dive Record

Dive No _____   Date _____

Dive Site _____

AIR

| START psi/bar | − | END psi/bar | = | psi/bar | × | CYLINDER CAPACITY | = | AIR USED | SURFACE AIR BREATHING RATE |

= _____ ltr per min

TIME

| SURFACE INTERVAL : | IN : | > | OUT : | = | DIVE DURATION | × | ABSOLUTE PRESSURE |

DECO - DEPTH

DECOMPRESSION / SAFETY STOPS

_____ mins at _____ m/ft _____ %

_____ mins at _____ m/ft _____ %

_____ mins at _____ m/ft _____ %

PRE DIVE GROUP   MAX DEPTH   END DIVE GROUP

Safety Margin: None 5% 10% 15% 20%

Computer / Decompression Tables Used: _____

WEIGHT

Weight Belt: _____ Kg/lbs

Integral BCD: _____ Kg/lbs

Ankle Weights: _____ Kg/lbs

Buoyancy: NEG - OK - POS

EXPOSURE

Suit: _____

Undersuit _____

Gloves _____

Hood _____

Assessment: COLD OK HOT

DCI RISK

Was this dive...
- Cold Water Dive ☐
- Decompression Dive ☐
- Deep Dive ☐
- Excessive Work ☐
- Missed Deco. Stops ☐
- Rapid Ascent ☐

Are you...
- Dehydrated ☐

TIDES

HIGH WATER :

LOW WATER :

SLACK WATER :

CURRENT _____ kn   DIRECTION _____ °

SEA CONDITIONS

SEA STATE

WATER TEMP

VISIBILITY

BEAUFORT SCALE

EQUIPMENT

Notes on additional equipment ...

Skipper _____   Boat _____

Accumulated Dive Time To Date	Dive Time this Dive	Total Dive Time To Date
:	:	:

Verification Signature   Certification No.

Dive Record

Dive No | **Date**

Dive Site

AIR

START psi/bar − END psi/bar = psi/bar × CYLINDER CAPACITY = AIR USED

SURFACE AIR BREATHING RATE = ltr per min

TIME

SURFACE INTERVAL : | IN : > OUT : = DIVE DURATION × ABSOLUTE PRESSURE

DECO - DEPTH

DECOMPRESSION / SAFETY STOPS
_____ mins at _____ m/ft _____ %
_____ mins at _____ m/ft _____ %
_____ mins at _____ m/ft _____ %

PRE DIVE GROUP | MAX DEPTH | END DIVE GROUP

Safety Margin: None 5% 10% 15% 20%

Computer / Decompression Tables Used:

WEIGHT

Weight Belt: _____ Kg/lbs

Integral BCD: _____ Kg/lbs

Ankle Weights: _____ Kg/lbs

Buoyancy: NEG - OK - POS

EXPOSURE

Suit: _____

Undersuit _____

Gloves _____

Hood _____

Assessment: COLD OK HOT

DCI RISK

Was this dive...
Cold Water Dive ☐
Decompression Dive ☐
Deep Dive ☐
Excessive Work ☐
Missed Deco. Stops ☐
Rapid Ascent ☐
Are you...
Dehydrated ☐

TIDES

HIGH WATER :

LOW WATER :

SLACK WATER :

CURRENT _____ kn   DIRECTION _____ °

SEA CONDITIONS

SEA STATE

WATER TEMP

VISIBILITY

BEAUFORT SCALE

EQUIPMENT

Notes on additional equipment ...

Skipper   Boat

Accumulated Dive Time To Date	Dive Time this Dive	Total Dive Time To Date
:	:	:

Verification Signature **Certification No.**

Dive Record

Dive No **Date**

Dive Site

AIR

| START psi/bar | − | END psi/bar | = | psi/bar | × | CYLINDER CAPACITY | = | AIR USED |

SURFACE AIR BREATHING RATE = ____ ltr per min

TIME

| SURFACE INTERVAL : | IN : | > | OUT : | = | DIVE DURATION | × | ABSOLUTE PRESSURE |

DECO - DEPTH

DECOMPRESSION / SAFETY STOPS
____ mins at ____ m/ft ____ %
____ mins at ____ m/ft ____ %
____ mins at ____ m/ft ____ %

PRE DIVE GROUP   MAX DEPTH   END DIVE GROUP

Safety Margin: None 5% 10% 15% 20%

Computer / Decompression Tables Used:

WEIGHT

Weight Belt: _____ Kg/lbs

Integral BCD: _____ Kg/lbs

Ankle Weights: _____ Kg/lbs

Buoyancy: NEG - OK - POS

EXPOSURE

Suit: _____
Undersuit _____
Gloves _____
Hood _____
Assessment: COLD OK HOT

DCI RISK

Was this dive...
Cold Water Dive ☐
Decompression Dive ☐
Deep Dive ☐
Excessive Work ☐
Missed Deco. Stops ☐
Rapid Ascent ☐
Are you...
Dehydrated ☐

TIDES

HIGH WATER :
LOW WATER :
SLACK WATER :
CURRENT ____ kn   DIRECTION ____ °

SEA CONDITIONS

SEA STATE
WATER TEMP
VISIBILITY
BEAUFORT SCALE

EQUIPMENT

Notes on additional equipment ...

Skipper **Boat**

Accumulated Dive Time To Date	Dive Time this Dive	Total Dive Time To Date
:	:	:

Verification Signature   **Certification No.**

Dive Record

Dive No **Date**

Dive Site

AIR

START psi/bar − END psi/bar = psi/bar × CYLINDER CAPACITY = AIR USED

SURFACE AIR BREATHING RATE

= ltr per min

TIME

SURFACE INTERVAL : | IN : > OUT : = DIVE DURATION × ABSOLUTE PRESSURE

DECO - DEPTH

DECOMPRESSION / SAFETY STOPS

_____ mins at _____ m/ft _____ %

_____ mins at _____ m/ft _____ %

_____ mins at _____ m/ft _____ %

PRE DIVE GROUP   MAX DEPTH   END DIVE GROUP

Safety Margin: None 5% 10% 15% 20%

Computer / Decompression Tables Used:

WEIGHT

Weight Belt: _____ Kg/lbs

Integral BCD: _____ Kg/lbs

Ankle Weights: _____ Kg/lbs

Buoyancy: NEG - OK - POS

EXPOSURE

Suit: _____

Undersuit _____

Gloves _____

Hood _____

Assessment: COLD OK HOT

DCI RISK

Was this dive...
Cold Water Dive ☐
Decompression Dive ☐
Deep Dive ☐
Excessive Work ☐
Missed Deco. Stops ☐
Rapid Ascent ☐
Are you...
Dehydrated ☐

TIDES

HIGH WATER :

LOW WATER :

SLACK WATER :

CURRENT _____ kn   DIRECTION _____ °

SEA CONDITIONS

SEA STATE

WATER TEMP

VISIBILITY

BEAUFORT SCALE

EQUIPMENT

Notes on additional equipment ...

Skipper **Boat**

Accumulated Dive Time To Date	Dive Time this Dive	Total Dive Time To Date
:	:	:

Verification Signature **Certification No.**

Dive Record

Dive No | Date

Dive Site

AIR
START psi/bar − END psi/bar = psi/bar × CYLINDER CAPACITY = AIR USED

SURFACE AIR BREATHING RATE = ltr per min

TIME
SURFACE INTERVAL : | IN : > OUT : = DIVE DURATION × ABSOLUTE PRESSURE

DECO - DEPTH
DECOMPRESSION / SAFETY STOPS

_____ mins at _____ m/ft _____ %

_____ mins at _____ m/ft _____ %

_____ mins at _____ m/ft _____ %

PRE DIVE GROUP | MAX DEPTH | END DIVE GROUP

Safety Margin: None 5% 10% 15% 20%

Computer / Decompression Tables Used:

WEIGHT

Weight Belt: _____ Kg/lbs

Integral BCD: _____ Kg/lbs

Ankle Weights: _____ Kg/lbs

Buoyancy: NEG - OK - POS

EXPOSURE

Suit: _____

Undersuit _____

Gloves _____

Hood _____

Assessment: COLD   OK   HOT

DCI RISK

Was this dive...
Cold Water Dive ☐
Decompression Dive ☐
Deep Dive ☐
Excessive Work ☐
Missed Deco. Stops ☐
Rapid Ascent ☐
Are you...
Dehydrated ☐

TIDES

HIGH WATER :

LOW WATER :

SLACK WATER :

CURRENT _____ kn   DIRECTION _____ °

SEA CONDITIONS

SEA STATE

WATER TEMP

VISIBILITY

BEAUFORT SCALE

EQUIPMENT

Notes on additional equipment ...

Skipper | Boat

Accumulated Dive Time To Date	Dive Time this Dive	Total Dive Time To Date
:	:	:

Verification Signature **Certification No.**

Dive Record

Dive No **Date**

Dive Site

AIR
| START psi/bar | − | END psi/bar | = | psi/bar | × | CYLINDER CAPACITY | = | AIR USED |

SURFACE AIR BREATHING RATE = ____ ltr per min

TIME
SURFACE INTERVAL : | IN : | > | OUT : | = | DIVE DURATION | × | ABSOLUTE PRESSURE

DECO - DEPTH
DECOMPRESSION / SAFETY STOPS
____ mins at ____ m/ft ____ %
____ mins at ____ m/ft ____ %
____ mins at ____ m/ft ____ %

PRE DIVE GROUP | MAX DEPTH | END DIVE GROUP

Safety Margin: None 5% 10% 15% 20%

Computer / Decompression Tables Used:

WEIGHT
Weight Belt: ____ Kg/lbs
Integral BCD: ____ Kg/lbs
Ankle Weights: ____ Kg/lbs
Buoyancy: NEG - OK - POS

EXPOSURE
Suit: ____
Undersuit ____
Gloves ____
Hood ____
Assessment: COLD OK HOT

DCI RISK
Was this dive...
Cold Water Dive ☐
Decompression Dive ☐
Deep Dive ☐
Excessive Work ☐
Missed Deco. Stops ☐
Rapid Ascent ☐
Are you...
Dehydrated ☐

TIDES
HIGH WATER :
LOW WATER :
SLACK WATER :
CURRENT ____ kn DIRECTION ____ °

SEA CONDITIONS
SEA STATE
WATER TEMP
VISIBILITY
BEAUFORT SCALE

EQUIPMENT
Notes on additional equipment ...

Skipper **Boat**

Accumulated Dive Time To Date	Dive Time this Dive	Total Dive Time To Date
:	:	:

Verification Signature   **Certification No.**

Dive Record

Dive No | **Date**

Dive Site

AIR
START psi/bar − END psi/bar = psi/bar × CYLINDER CAPACITY = AIR USED

SURFACE AIR BREATHING RATE = ltr per min

TIME
SURFACE INTERVAL : | IN : > OUT : = DIVE DURATION × ABSOLUTE PRESSURE

DECO - DEPTH
DECOMPRESSION / SAFETY STOPS
_____ mins at _____ m/ft _____ %
_____ mins at _____ m/ft _____ %
_____ mins at _____ m/ft _____ %

PRE DIVE GROUP | MAX DEPTH | END DIVE GROUP

Safety Margin: None 5% 10% 15% 20%

Computer / Decompression Tables Used:

WEIGHT
Weight Belt: _____ Kg/lbs
Integral BCD: _____ Kg/lbs
Ankle Weights: _____ Kg/lbs
Buoyancy: NEG - OK - POS

EXPOSURE
Suit: _____
Undersuit _____
Gloves _____
Hood _____
Assessment: COLD OK HOT

DCI RISK
Was this dive...
Cold Water Dive ☐
Decompression Dive ☐
Deep Dive ☐
Excessive Work ☐
Missed Deco. Stops ☐
Rapid Ascent ☐
Are you...
Dehydrated ☐

TIDES
HIGH WATER :
LOW WATER :
SLACK WATER :
CURRENT _____ kn   DIRECTION _____ °

SEA CONDITIONS
SEA STATE
WATER TEMP
VISIBILITY
BEAUFORT SCALE

EQUIPMENT
Notes on additional equipment ...

Skipper | **Boat**

Accumulated Dive Time To Date	Dive Time this Dive	Total Dive Time To Date
:	:	:

Verification Signature　　　　　　Certification No.

Dive Record

Dive No

Date

Dive Site

AIR

| START psi/bar | − | END psi/bar | = | psi/bar | × | CYLINDER CAPACITY | = | AIR USED | | SURFACE AIR BREATHING RATE |

= _____ ltr per min

TIME

| SURFACE INTERVAL : | | IN : | > | OUT : | = | DIVE DURATION | × | ABSOLUTE PRESSURE |

DECO - DEPTH

DECOMPRESSION / SAFETY STOPS

_____ mins at _____ m/ft _____ %

_____ mins at _____ m/ft _____ %

_____ mins at _____ m/ft _____ %

PRE DIVE GROUP

MAX DEPTH

END DIVE GROUP

Safety Margin: None 5% 10% 15% 20%

Computer / Decompression Tables Used:

WEIGHT

Weight Belt: _____ Kg/lbs

Integral BCD: _____ Kg/lbs

Ankle Weights: _____ Kg/lbs

Buoyancy: NEG - OK - POS

EXPOSURE

Suit: _____

Undersuit _____

Gloves _____

Hood _____

Assessment: COLD OK HOT

DCI RISK

Was this dive...
Cold Water Dive ☐
Decompression Dive ☐
Deep Dive ☐
Excessive Work ☐
Missed Deco. Stops ☐
Rapid Ascent ☐
Are you...
Dehydrated ☐

TIDES

HIGH WATER :

LOW WATER :

SLACK WATER :

CURRENT _____ kn   DIRECTION _____ °

SEA CONDITIONS

SEA STATE

WATER TEMP

VISIBILITY

BEAUFORT SCALE

EQUIPMENT

Notes on additional equipment ...

Skipper   Boat

Accumulated Dive Time To Date	Dive Time this Dive	Total Dive Time To Date
:	:	:

Verification Signature   **Certification No.**

Dive Record

Dive No

Date

Dive Site

AIR

| START psi/bar | − | END psi/bar | = | psi/bar | × | CYLINDER CAPACITY | = | AIR USED | | SURFACE AIR BREATHING RATE |

= _____ ltr per min

TIME

| SURFACE INTERVAL | | IN | > | OUT | = | DIVE DURATION | × | ABSOLUTE PRESSURE |

DECO - DEPTH

DECOMPRESSION / SAFETY STOPS

_____ mins at _____ m/ft _____ %
_____ mins at _____ m/ft _____ %
_____ mins at _____ m/ft _____ %

PRE DIVE GROUP

MAX DEPTH

END DIVE GROUP

Safety Margin: None 5% 10% 15% 20%

Computer / Decompression Tables Used:

WEIGHT

Weight Belt: _____ Kg/lbs

Integral BCD: _____ Kg/lbs

Ankle Weights: _____ Kg/lbs

Buoyancy: NEG - OK - POS

EXPOSURE

Suit: _____

Undersuit _____

Gloves _____

Hood _____

Assessment: COLD OK HOT

DCI RISK

Was this dive...
Cold Water Dive ☐
Decompression Dive ☐
Deep Dive ☐
Excessive Work ☐
Missed Deco. Stops ☐
Rapid Ascent ☐
Are you...
Dehydrated ☐

TIDES

HIGH WATER   :
LOW WATER   :
SLACK WATER   :
CURRENT _____ kn   DIRECTION _____ °

SEA CONDITIONS

SEA STATE

WATER TEMP

VISIBILITY

BEAUFORT SCALE

EQUIPMENT

Notes on additional equipment ...

Skipper   **Boat**

Accumulated Dive Time To Date	Dive Time this Dive	Total Dive Time To Date
:	:	:

Verification Signature   **Certification No.**

Dive Record

Dive No | Date

Dive Site

AIR: START psi/bar − END psi/bar = psi/bar × CYLINDER CAPACITY = AIR USED

SURFACE AIR BREATHING RATE = ltr per min

TIME: SURFACE INTERVAL : | IN : > OUT : = DIVE DURATION × ABSOLUTE PRESSURE

DECO - DEPTH:

DECOMPRESSION / SAFETY STOPS

____ mins at ____ m/ft ____ %
____ mins at ____ m/ft ____ %
____ mins at ____ m/ft ____ %

PRE DIVE GROUP | MAX DEPTH | END DIVE GROUP

Safety Margin: None 5% 10% 15% 20%

Computer / Decompression Tables Used:

WEIGHT

Weight Belt: _____ Kg/lbs
Integral BCD: _____ Kg/lbs
Ankle Weights: _____ Kg/lbs
Buoyancy: NEG - OK - POS

EXPOSURE

Suit: _____
Undersuit _____
Gloves _____
Hood _____
Assessment: COLD OK HOT

DCI RISK

Was this dive...
Cold Water Dive ☐
Decompression Dive ☐
Deep Dive ☐
Excessive Work ☐
Missed Deco. Stops ☐
Rapid Ascent ☐
Are you...
Dehydrated ☐

TIDES

HIGH WATER :
LOW WATER :
SLACK WATER :
CURRENT ____ kn   DIRECTION ____ °

SEA CONDITIONS

SEA STATE
WATER TEMP
VISIBILITY
BEAUFORT SCALE

EQUIPMENT

Notes on additional equipment ...

Skipper | Boat

Accumulated Dive Time To Date	Dive Time this Dive	Total Dive Time To Date
:	:	:

Verification Signature   Certification No.

Dive Record

Dive No | Date

Dive Site

AIR

| START psi/bar | − | END psi/bar | = | psi/bar | × | CYLINDER CAPACITY | = | AIR USED | SURFACE AIR BREATHING RATE |

= ltr per min

TIME

| SURFACE INTERVAL : | | IN : | > | OUT : | = | DIVE DURATION | × | ABSOLUTE PRESSURE |

DECO - DEPTH

DECOMPRESSION / SAFETY STOPS

____ mins at ____ m/ft ____ %
____ mins at ____ m/ft ____ %
____ mins at ____ m/ft ____ %

PRE DIVE GROUP | MAX DEPTH | END DIVE GROUP

Safety Margin: None 5% 10% 15% 20%

Computer / Decompression Tables Used:

WEIGHT

Weight Belt: ____ Kg/lbs

Integral BCD: ____ Kg/lbs

Ankle Weights: ____ Kg/lbs

Buoyancy: NEG - OK - POS

EXPOSURE

Suit: ____
Undersuit ____
Gloves ____
Hood ____
Assessment: COLD OK HOT

DCI RISK

Was this dive...
Cold Water Dive ☐
Decompression Dive ☐
Deep Dive ☐
Excessive Work ☐
Missed Deco. Stops ☐
Rapid Ascent ☐
Are you...
Dehydrated ☐

TIDES

HIGH WATER :
LOW WATER :
SLACK WATER :
CURRENT ____ kn DIRECTION ____ °

SEA CONDITIONS

SEA STATE
WATER TEMP
VISIBILITY
BEAUFORT SCALE

EQUIPMENT

Notes on additional equipment ...

Skipper   Boat

Accumulated Dive Time To Date	Dive Time this Dive	Total Dive Time To Date
:	:	:

Verification Signature   Certification No.

Dive Record

Dive No

Date

Dive Site

AIR

| START psi/bar | − | END psi/bar | = | psi/bar | × | CYLINDER CAPACITY | = | AIR USED |

SURFACE AIR BREATHING RATE = ____ ltr per min

TIME

| SURFACE INTERVAL : | | IN : | > | OUT : | = | DIVE DURATION | × | ABSOLUTE PRESSURE |

DECO - DEPTH

DECOMPRESSION / SAFETY STOPS

____ mins at ____ m/ft ____ %
____ mins at ____ m/ft ____ %
____ mins at ____ m/ft ____ %

PRE DIVE GROUP

MAX DEPTH

END DIVE GROUP

Safety Margin: None 5% 10% 15% 20%

Computer / Decompression Tables Used:

WEIGHT

Weight Belt: _____ Kg/lbs

Integral BCD: _____ Kg/lbs

Ankle Weights: _____ Kg/lbs

Buoyancy: NEG - OK - POS

EXPOSURE

Suit: _____

Undersuit _____

Gloves _____

Hood _____

Assessment: COLD OK HOT

DCI RISK

Was this dive...
Cold Water Dive ☐
Decompression Dive ☐
Deep Dive ☐
Excessive Work ☐
Missed Deco. Stops ☐
Rapid Ascent ☐
Are you...
Dehydrated ☐

TIDES

HIGH WATER :

LOW WATER :

SLACK WATER :

CURRENT ____ kn   DIRECTION ____ °

SEA CONDITIONS

SEA STATE

WATER TEMP

VISIBILITY

BEAUFORT SCALE

EQUIPMENT

Notes on additional equipment ...

_____
_____
_____
_____
_____

Skipper   **Boat**

Accumulated Dive Time To Date	Dive Time this Dive	Total Dive Time To Date
:	:	:

Verification Signature   Certification No.

Dive Record

Dive No | **Date**

Dive Site

AIR
START psi/bar − END psi/bar = psi/bar × CYLINDER CAPACITY = AIR USED

SURFACE AIR BREATHING RATE = ltr per min

TIME
SURFACE INTERVAL : | IN : > OUT : = DIVE DURATION × ABSOLUTE PRESSURE

DECO DEPTH
DECOMPRESSION / SAFETY STOPS
_____ mins at _____ m/ft _____ %
_____ mins at _____ m/ft _____ %
_____ mins at _____ m/ft _____ %

PRE DIVE GROUP | MAX DEPTH | END DIVE GROUP

Safety Margin: None 5% 10% 15% 20%

Computer / Decompression Tables Used:

WEIGHT

Weight Belt: _____ Kg/lbs

Integral BCD: _____ Kg/lbs

Ankle Weights: _____ Kg/lbs

Buoyancy: NEG - OK - POS

EXPOSURE

Suit: _____

Undersuit _____

Gloves _____

Hood _____

Assessment: COLD OK HOT

DCI RISK

Was this dive...
Cold Water Dive ☐
Decompression Dive ☐
Deep Dive ☐
Excessive Work ☐
Missed Deco. Stops ☐
Rapid Ascent ☐
Are you...
Dehydrated ☐

TIDES

HIGH WATER :

LOW WATER :

SLACK WATER :

CURRENT _____ kn   DIRECTION _____ °

SEA CONDITIONS

SEA STATE

WATER TEMP

VISIBILITY

BEAUFORT SCALE

EQUIPMENT

Notes on additional equipment ...

Skipper | **Boat**

Accumulated Dive Time To Date	Dive Time this Dive	Total Dive Time To Date
:	:	:

Verification Signature   Certification No.

Dive Record

Dive No   **Date**

Dive Site

AIR

| START psi/bar | − | END psi/bar | = | psi/bar | × | CYLINDER CAPACITY | = | AIR USED | | SURFACE AIR BREATHING RATE |

= _____ ltr per min

TIME

| SURFACE INTERVAL : | > | IN : | > | OUT : | = | DIVE DURATION | × | ABSOLUTE PRESSURE |

DECO - DEPTH

DECOMPRESSION / SAFETY STOPS

_____ mins at _____ m/ft _____ %
_____ mins at _____ m/ft _____ %
_____ mins at _____ m/ft _____ %

| PRE DIVE GROUP | MAX DEPTH | END DIVE GROUP |

Safety Margin: None   5%   10%   15%   20%

Computer / Decompression Tables Used:

WEIGHT

Weight Belt: _____ Kg/lbs

Integral BCD: _____ Kg/lbs

Ankle Weights: _____ Kg/lbs

Buoyancy: NEG - OK - POS

EXPOSURE

Suit: _____

Undersuit _____

Gloves _____

Hood _____

Assessment: COLD   OK   HOT

DCI RISK

Was this dive...
Cold Water Dive ☐
Decompression Dive ☐
Deep Dive ☐
Excessive Work ☐
Missed Deco. Stops ☐
Rapid Ascent ☐
Are you...
Dehydrated ☐

TIDES

HIGH WATER :

LOW WATER :

SLACK WATER :

CURRENT _____ kn   DIRECTION _____ °

SEA CONDITIONS

SEA STATE

WATER TEMP

VISIBILITY

BEAUFORT SCALE

EQUIPMENT

Notes on additional equipment ...

Skipper   **Boat**

Accumulated Dive Time To Date	Dive Time this Dive	Total Dive Time To Date
:	:	:

Verification Signature **Certification No.**

Dive Record

Dive No

Date

Dive Site

AIR

| START psi/bar | − | END psi/bar | = | psi/bar | × | CYLINDER CAPACITY | = | AIR USED |

SURFACE AIR BREATHING RATE

= _____ ltr per min

TIME

| SURFACE INTERVAL : | | IN : | > | OUT : | = | DIVE DURATION | × | ABSOLUTE PRESSURE |

DECO - DEPTH

DECOMPRESSION / SAFETY STOPS

_____ mins at _____ m/ft _____ %

_____ mins at _____ m/ft _____ %

_____ mins at _____ m/ft _____ %

PRE DIVE GROUP

MAX DEPTH

END DIVE GROUP

Safety Margin. None 5% 10% 15% 20%

Computer / Decompression Tables Used:

WEIGHT

Weight Belt: _____ Kg/lbs

Integral BCD: _____ Kg/lbs

Ankle Weights: _____ Kg/lbs

Buoyancy: NEG - OK - POS

EXPOSURE

Suit: _____

Undersuit _____

Gloves _____

Hood _____

Assessment: COLD OK HOT

DCI RISK

Was this dive...
Cold Water Dive ☐
Decompression Dive ☐
Deep Dive ☐
Excessive Work ☐
Missed Deco. Stops ☐
Rapid Ascent ☐
Are you...
Dehydrated ☐

TIDES

HIGH WATER :

LOW WATER :

SLACK WATER :

CURRENT _____ kn   DIRECTION _____ °

SEA CONDITIONS

SEA STATE

WATER TEMP

VISIBILITY

BEAUFORT SCALE

EQUIPMENT

Notes on additional equipment ...

Skipper

Boat

Accumulated Dive Time To Date	Dive Time this Dive	Total Dive Time To Date
:	:	:

Verification Signature   **Certification No.**

Dive Record

Dive No **Date**

Dive Site

AIR
| START psi/bar | − | END psi/bar | = | psi/bar | × | CYLINDER CAPACITY | = | AIR USED | SURFACE AIR BREATHING RATE |

= ltr per min

TIME
SURFACE INTERVAL : | IN : | > | OUT : | = | DIVE DURATION | × | ABSOLUTE PRESSURE

DECO - DEPTH

DECOMPRESSION / SAFETY STOPS

_____ mins at _____ m/ft _____ %

_____ mins at _____ m/ft _____ %

_____ mins at _____ m/ft _____ %

PRE DIVE GROUP | MAX DEPTH | END DIVE GROUP

Safety Margin: None 5% 10% 15% 20%

Computer / Decompression Tables Used:

WEIGHT

Weight Belt: _____ Kg/lbs

Integral BCD: _____ Kg/lbs

Ankle Weights: _____ Kg/lbs

Buoyancy: NEG - OK - POS

EXPOSURE

Suit: _____

Undersuit _____

Gloves _____

Hood _____

Assessment: COLD OK HOT

DCI RISK

Was this dive...
Cold Water Dive ☐
Decompression Dive ☐
Deep Dive ☐
Excessive Work ☐
Missed Deco. Stops ☐
Rapid Ascent ☐
Are you...
Dehydrated ☐

TIDES

HIGH WATER :

LOW WATER :

SLACK WATER :

CURRENT _____ kn DIRECTION _____ °

SEA CONDITIONS

SEA STATE

WATER TEMP

VISIBILITY

BEAUFORT SCALE

EQUIPMENT

Notes on additional equipment ...

_____

_____

_____

_____

Skipper **Boat**

Accumulated Dive Time To Date	Dive Time this Dive	Total Dive Time To Date
:	:	:

Verification Signature   Certification No.

Dive Record

Dive No **Date**

Dive Site

AIR
| START psi/bar | − | END psi/bar | = | psi/bar | × | CYLINDER CAPACITY | = | AIR USED | SURFACE AIR BREATHING RATE |

= _____ ltr per min

TIME
| SURFACE INTERVAL : | | IN : | > | OUT : | = | DIVE DURATION | × | ABSOLUTE PRESSURE |

DECO - DEPTH

DECOMPRESSION / SAFETY STOPS

____ mins at ____ m/ft ____ %
____ mins at ____ m/ft ____ %
____ mins at ____ m/ft ____ %

| PRE DIVE GROUP | MAX DEPTH | END DIVE GROUP |

Safety Margin: None 3% 10% 15% 20%

Computer / Decompression Tables Used:

WEIGHT

Weight Belt: _____ Kg/lbs

Integral BCD: _____ Kg/lbs

Ankle Weights: _____ Kg/lbs

Buoyancy: NEG - OK - POS

EXPOSURE

Suit: _____

Undersuit _____

Gloves _____

Hood _____

Assessment: COLD OK HOT

DCI RISK

Was this dive...
Cold Water Dive ☐
Decompression Dive ☐
Deep Dive ☐
Excessive Work ☐
Missed Deco. Stops ☐
Rapid Ascent ☐
Are you...
Dehydrated ☐

TIDES

HIGH WATER :

LOW WATER :

SLACK WATER :

CURRENT ____ kn   DIRECTION ____ °

SEA CONDITIONS

SEA STATE

WATER TEMP

VISIBILITY

BEAUFORT SCALE

EQUIPMENT

Notes on additional equipment ...

Skipper   **Boat**

Accumulated Dive Time To Date	Dive Time this Dive	Total Dive Time To Date
:	:	:

Verification Signature   Certification No.

Dive Record

Dive No | **Date**

Dive Site

AIR
START psi/bar − END psi/bar = psi/bar × CYLINDER CAPACITY = AIR USED

SURFACE AIR BREATHING RATE = ltr per min

TIME
SURFACE INTERVAL : | IN : > OUT : = DIVE DURATION × ABSOLUTE PRESSURE

DECO - DEPTH
DECOMPRESSION / SAFETY STOPS
____mins at ____m/ft ____%
____mins at ____m/ft ____%
____mins at ____m/ft ____%

PRE DIVE GROUP | MAX DEPTH | END DIVE GROUP

Safety Margin: None 5% 10% 15% 20%

Computer / Decompression Tables Used:

WEIGHT

Weight Belt: _____ Kg/lbs

Integral BCD: _____ Kg/lbs

Ankle Weights: _____ Kg/lbs

Buoyancy: NEG - OK - POS

EXPOSURE

Suit: _____

Undersuit _____

Gloves _____

Hood _____

Assessment: COLD OK HOT

DCI RISK

Was this dive...
- Cold Water Dive ☐
- Decompression Dive ☐
- Deep Dive ☐
- Excessive Work ☐
- Missed Deco. Stops ☐
- Rapid Ascent ☐

Are you...
- Dehydrated ☐

TIDES

HIGH WATER :

LOW WATER :

SLACK WATER :

CURRENT ____kn DIRECTION ____°

SEA CONDITIONS

SEA STATE

WATER TEMP

VISIBILITY

BEAUFORT SCALE

EQUIPMENT

Notes on additional equipment ...

Skipper | **Boat**

Accumulated Dive Time To Date	Dive Time this Dive	Total Dive Time To Date
:	:	:

Verification Signature Certification No.

Dive Record

Dive No | **Date**

Dive Site

AIR

START psi/bar − END psi/bar = psi/bar × CYLINDER CAPACITY = AIR USED

SURFACE AIR BREATHING RATE = ltr per min

TIME

SURFACE INTERVAL : | IN : | > OUT : | = DIVE DURATION | × ABSOLUTE PRESSURE

DECO - DEPTH

DECOMPRESSION / SAFETY STOPS

_____ mins at _____ m/ft _____ %

_____ mins at _____ m/ft _____ %

_____ mins at _____ m/ft _____ %

PRE DIVE GROUP | MAX DEPTH | END DIVE GROUP

Safety Margin: None 5% 10% 15% 20%

Computer / Decompression Tables Used:

WEIGHT

Weight Belt: _____ Kg/lbs

Integral BCD: _____ Kg/lbs

Ankle Weights: _____ Kg/lbs

Buoyancy: NEG - OK - POS

EXPOSURE

Suit: _____

Undersuit _____

Gloves _____

Hood _____

Assessment: COLD OK HOT

DCI RISK

Was this dive...
Cold Water Dive ☐
Decompression Dive ☐
Deep Dive ☐
Excessive Work ☐
Missed Deco. Stops ☐
Rapid Ascent ☐
Are you...
Dehydrated ☐

TIDES

HIGH WATER :

LOW WATER :

SLACK WATER :

CURRENT _____ kn DIRECTION _____ °

SEA CONDITIONS

SEA STATE

WATER TEMP

VISIBILITY

BEAUFORT SCALE

EQUIPMENT

Notes on additional equipment ...

Skipper | **Boat**

Accumulated Dive Time To Date	Dive Time this Dive	Total Dive Time To Date
:	:	:

Verification Signature · Certification No.

Dive Record

Dive No | **Date**

Dive Site

AIR
START psi/bar − END psi/bar = psi/bar × CYLINDER CAPACITY = AIR USED

SURFACE AIR BREATHING RATE = ltr per min

TIME
SURFACE INTERVAL : | IN : > OUT : = DIVE DURATION × ABSOLUTE PRESSURE

DECO - DEPTH

DECOMPRESSION / SAFETY STOPS
_____ mins at _____ m/ft _____ %
_____ mins at _____ m/ft _____ %
_____ mins at _____ m/ft _____ %

PRE DIVE GROUP | MAX DEPTH | END DIVE GROUP

Safety Margin: None 5% 10% 15% 20%

Computer / Decompression Tables Used:

WEIGHT

Weight Belt: _____ Kg/lbs
Integral BCD: _____ Kg/lbs
Ankle Weights: _____ Kg/lbs
Buoyancy: NEG - OK - POS

EXPOSURE

Suit: _____
Undersuit _____
Gloves _____
Hood _____
Assessment: COLD OK HOT

DCI RISK

Was this dive...
Cold Water Dive ☐
Decompression Dive ☐
Deep Dive ☐
Excessive Work ☐
Missed Deco. Stops ☐
Rapid Ascent ☐
Are you...
Dehydrated ☐

TIDES

HIGH WATER :
LOW WATER :
SLACK WATER :
CURRENT _____ kn   DIRECTION _____ °

SEA CONDITIONS

SEA STATE
WATER TEMP
VISIBILITY
BEAUFORT SCALE

EQUIPMENT

Notes on additional equipment ...

Skipper | **Boat**

Accumulated Dive Time To Date	Dive Time this Dive	Total Dive Time To Date
:	:	:

Verification Signature Certification No.

Dive Record

Dive No | Date

Dive Site

AIR
| START psi/bar | − | END psi/bar | = | psi/bar | × | CYLINDER CAPACITY | = | AIR USED |

SURFACE AIR BREATHING RATE
= ltr per min

TIME
| SURFACE INTERVAL : | | IN : | > | OUT : | = | DIVE DURATION | × | ABSOLUTE PRESSURE |

DECO - DEPTH

DECOMPRESSION / SAFETY STOPS
_____ mins at _____ m/ft _____ %
_____ mins at _____ m/ft _____ %
_____ mins at _____ m/ft _____ %

PRE DIVE GROUP | MAX DEPTH | END DIVE GROUP

Safety Margin: None 5% 10% 15% 20%

Computer / Decompression Tables Used:

WEIGHT

Weight Belt: _____ Kg/lbs

Integral BCD: _____ Kg/lbs

Ankle Weights: _____ Kg/lbs

Buoyancy: NEG - OK - POS

EXPOSURE

Suit: _____

Undersuit _____

Gloves _____

Hood _____

Assessment: COLD OK HOT

DCI RISK

Was this dive...
Cold Water Dive ☐
Decompression Dive ☐
Deep Dive ☐
Excessive Work ☐
Missed Deco. Stops ☐
Rapid Ascent ☐
Are you...
Dehydrated ☐

TIDES

HIGH WATER :

LOW WATER :

SLACK WATER :

CURRENT _____ kn | DIRECTION _____ °

SEA CONDITIONS

SEA STATE

WATER TEMP

VISIBILITY

BEAUFORT SCALE

EQUIPMENT

Notes on additional equipment ...

Skipper | Boat

Accumulated Dive Time To Date	Dive Time this Dive	Total Dive Time To Date
:	:	:

Verification Signature   **Certification No.**

Dive Record

Dive No   **Date**

Dive Site

AIR

| START psi/bar | − | END psi/bar | = | psi/bar | × | CYLINDER CAPACITY | = | AIR USED | SURFACE AIR BREATHING RATE |

= ltr per min

TIME

| SURFACE INTERVAL : | IN : | > | OUT : | = | DIVE DURATION | × | ABSOLUTE PRESSURE |

DECO - DEPTH

DECOMPRESSION / SAFETY STOPS

_____ mins at _____ m/ft _____ %

_____ mins at _____ m/ft _____ %

_____ mins at _____ m/ft _____ %

PRE DIVE GROUP   MAX DEPTH   END DIVE GROUP

Safety Margin: None 5% 10% 15% 20%

Computer / Decompression Tables Used:

WEIGHT

Weight Belt: _____ Kg/lbs

Integral BCD: _____ Kg/lbs

Ankle Weights: _____ Kg/lbs

Buoyancy: NEG - OK - POS

EXPOSURE

Suit: _____

Undersuit _____

Gloves _____

Hood _____

Assessment: COLD OK HOT

DCI RISK

Was this dive...
- Cold Water Dive ☐
- Decompression Dive ☐
- Deep Dive ☐
- Excessive Work ☐
- Missed Deco. Stops ☐
- Rapid Ascent ☐

Are you...
- Dehydrated ☐

TIDES

HIGH WATER :

LOW WATER :

SLACK WATER :

CURRENT _____ kn   DIRECTION _____ °

SEA CONDITIONS

SEA STATE

WATER TEMP

VISIBILITY

BEAUFORT SCALE

EQUIPMENT

Notes on additional equipment ...

Skipper   **Boat**

Accumulated Dive Time To Date	Dive Time this Dive	Total Dive Time To Date
:	:	:

Verification Signature **Certification No.**

Dive Record

Dive No | **Date**

Dive Site

AIR: START psi/bar − END psi/bar = psi/bar × CYLINDER CAPACITY = AIR USED | SURFACE AIR BREATHING RATE = ltr per min

TIME: SURFACE INTERVAL : | IN : | OUT : | DIVE DURATION = | ABSOLUTE PRESSURE ×

DECO - DEPTH:

DECOMPRESSION / SAFETY STOPS
____ mins at ____ m/ft ____ %
____ mins at ____ m/ft ____ %
____ mins at ____ m/ft ____ %

PRE DIVE GROUP | MAX DEPTH | END DIVE GROUP

Safety Margin: None 5% 10% 15% 20%

Computer / Decompression Tables Used:

WEIGHT

Weight Belt: _____ Kg/lbs

Integral BCD: _____ Kg/lbs

Ankle Weights: _____ Kg/lbs

Buoyancy: NEG - OK - POS

EXPOSURE

Suit: _____

Undersuit _____

Gloves _____

Hood _____

Assessment: COLD OK HOT

DCI RISK

Was this dive...
Cold Water Dive ☐
Decompression Dive ☐
Deep Dive ☐
Excessive Work ☐
Missed Deco. Stops ☐
Rapid Ascent ☐
Are you...
Dehydrated ☐

TIDES

HIGH WATER :

LOW WATER :

SLACK WATER :

CURRENT ____ kn   DIRECTION ____ °

SEA CONDITIONS

SEA STATE

WATER TEMP

VISIBILITY

BEAUFORT SCALE

EQUIPMENT

Notes on additional equipment ...

Skipper | Boat

Accumulated Dive Time To Date	Dive Time this Dive	Total Dive Time To Date
:	:	:

Verification Signature **Certification No.**

Dive Record

Dive No | Date

Dive Site

AIR: START psi/bar − END psi/bar = psi/bar × CYLINDER CAPACITY = AIR USED

SURFACE AIR BREATHING RATE = ___ ltr per min

TIME: SURFACE INTERVAL : | IN : > OUT : = DIVE DURATION × ABSOLUTE PRESSURE

DECO - DEPTH: DECOMPRESSION / SAFETY STOPS
____ mins at ____ m/ft ____ %
____ mins at ____ m/ft ____ %
____ mins at ____ m/ft ____ %

PRE DIVE GROUP | MAX DEPTH | END DIVE GROUP

Safety Margin: None 5% 10% 15% 20%

Computer / Decompression Tables Used:

WEIGHT

Weight Belt: ____ Kg/lbs
Integral BCD: ____ Kg/lbs
Ankle Weights: ____ Kg/lbs
Buoyancy: NEG - OK - POS

EXPOSURE

Suit: ____
Undersuit ____
Gloves ____
Hood ____
Assessment: COLD OK HOT

DCI RISK

Was this dive...
- Cold Water Dive ☐
- Decompression Dive ☐
- Deep Dive ☐
- Excessive Work ☐
- Missed Deco. Stops ☐
- Rapid Ascent ☐

Are you...
- Dehydrated ☐

TIDES

HIGH WATER :
LOW WATER :
SLACK WATER :
CURRENT ____ kn DIRECTION ____ °

SEA CONDITIONS

SEA STATE
WATER TEMP
VISIBILITY
BEAUFORT SCALE

EQUIPMENT

Notes on additional equipment ...

Skipper | Boat

Accumulated Dive Time To Date	Dive Time this Dive	Total Dive Time To Date
:	:	:

Verification Signature **Certification No.**

Dive Record

Dive No | **Date**

Dive Site

AIR

START psi/bar − END psi/bar = psi/bar × CYLINDER CAPACITY = AIR USED / SURFACE AIR BREATHING RATE = ltr per min

TIME

SURFACE INTERVAL : | IN : > OUT : = DIVE DURATION × ABSOLUTE PRESSURE

DECO - DEPTH

DECOMPRESSION / SAFETY STOPS

_____ mins at _____ m/ft _____ %

_____ mins at _____ m/ft _____ %

_____ mins at _____ m/ft _____ %

PRE DIVE GROUP | MAX DEPTH | END DIVE GROUP

Safety Margin: None 5% 10% 15% 20%

Computer / Decompression Tables Used:

WEIGHT

Weight Belt: _____ Kg/lbs

Integral BCD: _____ Kg/lbs

Ankle Weights: _____ Kg/lbs

Buoyancy: NEG - OK - POS

EXPOSURE

Suit: _____

Undersuit _____

Gloves _____

Hood _____

Assessment: COLD OK HOT

DCI RISK

Was this dive...
Cold Water Dive ☐
Decompression Dive ☐
Deep Dive ☐
Excessive Work ☐
Missed Deco. Stops ☐
Rapid Ascent ☐
Are you...
Dehydrated ☐

TIDES

HIGH WATER :

LOW WATER :

SLACK WATER :

CURRENT _____ kn   DIRECTION _____ °

SEA CONDITIONS

SEA STATE

WATER TEMP

VISIBILITY

BEAUFORT SCALE

EQUIPMENT

Notes on additional equipment ...

_____
_____
_____
_____
_____

Skipper | **Boat**

Accumulated Dive Time To Date	Dive Time this Dive	Total Dive Time To Date
:	:	:

Verification Signature   Certification No.

Dive Record

Dive No
Date
Dive Site

AIR

| START psi/bar | − | END psi/bar | = | psi/bar | × | CYLINDER CAPACITY | = | AIR USED | SURFACE AIR BREATHING RATE |

_____ ltr per min

TIME

SURFACE INTERVAL :

IN : > OUT : = DIVE DURATION × ABSOLUTE PRESSURE =

DECO - DEPTH

DECOMPRESSION / SAFETY STOPS

_____ mins at _____ m/ft _____ %
_____ mins at _____ m/ft _____ %
_____ mins at _____ m/ft _____ %

PRE DIVE GROUP   MAX DEPTH   END DIVE GROUP

Safety Margin: None 5% 10% 15% 20%

Computer / Decompression Tables Used:

WEIGHT

Weight Belt: _____ Kg/lbs
Integral BCD: _____ Kg/lbs
Ankle Weights: _____ Kg/lbs
Buoyancy: NEG - OK - POS

EXPOSURE

Suit: _____
Undersuit _____
Gloves _____
Hood _____
Assessment: COLD OK HOT

DCI RISK

Was this dive...
Cold Water Dive ☐
Decompression Dive ☐
Deep Dive ☐
Excessive Work ☐
Missed Deco. Stops ☐
Rapid Ascent ☐
Are you...
Dehydrated ☐

TIDES

HIGH WATER :
LOW WATER :
SLACK WATER :
CURRENT _____ kn   DIRECTION _____ °

SEA CONDITIONS

SEA STATE
WATER TEMP
VISIBILITY
BEAUFORT SCALE

EQUIPMENT

Notes on additional equipment ...

Skipper   **Boat**

Accumulated Dive Time To Date	Dive Time this Dive	Total Dive Time To Date
:	:	:

Verification SignatureCertification No.

Dive Record

Dive No | Date

Dive Site

AIR: START psi/bar − END psi/bar = psi/bar × CYLINDER CAPACITY = AIR USED

SURFACE AIR BREATHING RATE = ltr per min

TIME: SURFACE INTERVAL : | IN : > OUT : = DIVE DURATION × ABSOLUTE PRESSURE

DECO - DEPTH: DECOMPRESSION / SAFETY STOPS
____mins at _____m/ft _____%
____mins at _____m/ft _____%
____mins at _____m/ft _____%

PRE DIVE GROUP | MAX DEPTH | END DIVE GROUP

Safety Margin: None 5% 10% 15% 20%

Computer / Decompression Tables Used:

WEIGHT

Weight Belt: _____ Kg/lbs

Integral BCD: _____ Kg/lbs

Ankle Weights: _____ Kg/lbs

Buoyancy: NEG - OK - POS

EXPOSURE

Suit: _____

Undersuit _____

Gloves _____

Hood _____

Assessment: COLD OK HOT

DCI RISK

Was this dive...
Cold Water Dive ☐
Decompression Dive ☐
Deep Dive ☐
Excessive Work ☐
Missed Deco. Stops ☐
Rapid Ascent ☐
Are you...
Dehydrated ☐

TIDES

HIGH WATER :

LOW WATER :

SLACK WATER :

CURRENT _____kn DIRECTION _____°

SEA CONDITIONS

SEA STATE

WATER TEMP

VISIBILITY

BEAUFORT SCALE

EQUIPMENT

Notes on additional equipment ...

Skipper | Boat

Accumulated Dive Time To Date	Dive Time this Dive	Total Dive Time To Date
:	:	:

Verification Signature Certification No.

Dive Record

Dive No   **Date**

Dive Site

AIR

| START psi/bar | − | END psi/bar | = | psi/bar | × | CYLINDER CAPACITY | = | AIR USED | / SURFACE AIR BREATHING RATE |

= _____ ltr per min

TIME

| SURFACE INTERVAL : | IN : | > | OUT : | = | DIVE DURATION | × | ABSOLUTE PRESSURE |

DECO - DEPTH

DECOMPRESSION / SAFETY STOPS

_____ mins at _____ m/ft _____ %
_____ mins at _____ m/ft _____ %
_____ mins at _____ m/ft _____ %

PRE DIVE GROUP   MAX DEPTH   END DIVE GROUP

Safety Margin: None   5%   10%   15%   20%

Computer / Decompression Tables Used:

WEIGHT

Weight Belt: _____ Kg/lbs

Integral BCD: _____ Kg/lbs

Ankle Weights: _____ Kg/lbs

Buoyancy: NEG - OK - POS

EXPOSURE

Suit: _____

Undersuit _____

Gloves _____

Hood _____

Assessment: COLD   OK   HOT

DCI RISK

Was this dive...
Cold Water Dive ☐
Decompression Dive ☐
Deep Dive ☐
Excessive Work ☐
Missed Deco. Stops ☐
Rapid Ascent ☐
Are you...
Dehydrated ☐

TIDES

HIGH WATER	:
LOW WATER	:
SLACK WATER	:

CURRENT _____ kn   DIRECTION _____ °

SEA CONDITIONS

SEA STATE

WATER TEMP

VISIBILITY

BEAUFORT SCALE

EQUIPMENT

Notes on additional equipment ...

Skipper   **Boat**

Accumulated Dive Time To Date	Dive Time this Dive	Total Dive Time To Date
:	:	:

Verification Signature **Certification No.**

Dive Record

Dive No Date

Dive Site

AIR
START psi/bar − END psi/bar = psi/bar × CYLINDER CAPACITY = AIR USED

SURFACE AIR BREATHING RATE
= ltr per min

TIME
SURFACE INTERVAL : | IN : | OUT : | DIVE DURATION | × ABSOLUTE PRESSURE

DECO - DEPTH
DECOMPRESSION / SAFETY STOPS
_____ mins at _____ m/ft _____ %
_____ mins at _____ m/ft _____ %
_____ mins at _____ m/ft _____ %

PRE DIVE GROUP | MAX DEPTH | END DIVE GROUP

Safety Margin: None 5% 10% 15% 20%

Computer / Decompression Tables Used:

WEIGHT

Weight Belt: _____ Kg/lbs
Integral BCD: _____ Kg/lbs
Ankle Weights: _____ Kg/lbs
Buoyancy: NEG - OK - POS

EXPOSURE

Suit: _____
Undersuit _____
Gloves _____
Hood _____
Assessment: COLD OK HOT

DCI RISK

Was this dive...
Cold Water Dive ☐
Decompression Dive ☐
Deep Dive ☐
Excessive Work ☐
Missed Deco. Stops ☐
Rapid Ascent ☐
Are you...
Dehydrated ☐

TIDES

HIGH WATER :
LOW WATER :
SLACK WATER :
CURRENT _____ kn   DIRECTION _____ °

SEA CONDITIONS

SEA STATE

WATER TEMP

VISIBILITY

BEAUFORT SCALE

EQUIPMENT

Notes on additional equipment ...

Skipper Boat

Accumulated Dive Time To Date	Dive Time this Dive	Total Dive Time To Date
:	:	:

Verification Signature   **Certification No.**

Dive Record

Dive No | **Date**

Dive Site

AIR
| START psi/bar | − | END psi/bar | = | psi/bar | × | CYLINDER CAPACITY | = | AIR USED | / | SURFACE AIR BREATHING RATE = ltr per min |

TIME
| SURFACE INTERVAL : | IN : | > | OUT : | = | DIVE DURATION | × | ABSOLUTE PRESSURE |

DECO - DEPTH
DECOMPRESSION / SAFETY STOPS
____ mins at ____ m/ft ____ %
____ mins at ____ m/ft ____ %
____ mins at ____ m/ft ____ %

PRE DIVE GROUP | MAX DEPTH | END DIVE GROUP

Safety Margin: None 5% 10% 15% 20%

Computer / Decompression Tables Used:

WEIGHT

Weight Belt: _____ Kg/lbs

Integral BCD: _____ Kg/lbs

Ankle Weights: _____ Kg/lbs

Buoyancy: NEG - OK - POS

EXPOSURE

Suit: _____

Undersuit _____

Gloves _____

Hood _____

Assessment: COLD OK HOT

DCI RISK

Was this dive...
Cold Water Dive ☐
Decompression Dive ☐
Deep Dive ☐
Excessive Work ☐
Missed Deco. Stops ☐
Rapid Ascent ☐
Are you...
Dehydrated ☐

TIDES

HIGH WATER :

LOW WATER :

SLACK WATER :

CURRENT ____ kn   DIRECTION ____ °

SEA CONDITIONS

SEA STATE

WATER TEMP

VISIBILITY

BEAUFORT SCALE

EQUIPMENT

Notes on additional equipment ...

Skipper | **Boat**

Accumulated Dive Time To Date	Dive Time this Dive	Total Dive Time To Date
:	:	:

Verification Signature Certification No.

Dive Record

Dive No | **Date**

Dive Site

AIR

| START psi/bar | − | END psi/bar | = | psi/bar | × | CYLINDER CAPACITY | = | AIR USED | SURFACE AIR BREATHING RATE |

= ltr per min

TIME

| SURFACE INTERVAL : | IN : | > | OUT : | = | DIVE DURATION | × | ABSOLUTE PRESSURE |

DECO - DEPTH

DECOMPRESSION / SAFETY STOPS

_____ mins at _____ m/ft _____ %
_____ mins at _____ m/ft _____ %
_____ mins at _____ m/ft _____ %

PRE DIVE GROUP | MAX DEPTH | END DIVE GROUP

Safety Margin: None 5% 10% 15% 20%

Computer / Decompression Tables Used:

WEIGHT

Weight Belt: _____ Kg/lbs

Integral BCD: _____ Kg/lbs

Ankle Weights: _____ Kg/lbs

Buoyancy: NEG - OK - POS

EXPOSURE

Suit: _____

Undersuit _____

Gloves _____

Hood _____

Assessment: COLD OK HOT

DCI RISK

Was this dive...
Cold Water Dive ☐
Decompression Dive ☐
Deep Dive ☐
Excessive Work ☐
Missed Deco. Stops ☐
Rapid Ascent ☐
Are you...
Dehydrated ☐

TIDES

HIGH WATER	:
LOW WATER	:
SLACK WATER	:

CURRENT _____ kn DIRECTION _____ °

SEA CONDITIONS

SEA STATE

WATER TEMP

VISIBILITY

BEAUFORT SCALE

EQUIPMENT

Notes on additional equipment ...

_____
_____
_____
_____
_____

Skipper | Boat

Accumulated Dive Time To Date	Dive Time this Dive	Total Dive Time To Date
:	:	:

Verification Signature Certification No.

Dive Record

Dive No | **Date**

Dive Site

AIR

| START psi/bar | − | END psi/bar | = | psi/bar | × | CYLINDER CAPACITY | = | AIR USED | / | SURFACE AIR BREATHING RATE = ltr per min |

TIME

| SURFACE INTERVAL : | | IN : | > | OUT : | = | DIVE DURATION | × | ABSOLUTE PRESSURE |

DECO - DEPTH

DECOMPRESSION / SAFETY STOPS

____ mins at ____ m/ft ____ %
____ mins at ____ m/ft ____ %
____ mins at ____ m/ft ____ %

PRE DIVE GROUP | MAX DEPTH | END DIVE GROUP

Safety Margin: None 5% 10% 15% 20%

Computer / Decompression Tables Used:

WEIGHT

Weight Belt: _____ Kg/lbs

Integral BCD: _____ Kg/lbs

Ankle Weights: _____ Kg/lbs

Buoyancy: NEG - OK - POS

EXPOSURE

Suit: _____

Undersuit _____

Gloves _____

Hood _____

Assessment: COLD OK HOT

DCI RISK

Was this dive...
Cold Water Dive ☐
Decompression Dive ☐
Deep Dive ☐
Excessive Work ☐
Missed Deco. Stops ☐
Rapid Ascent ☐
Are you...
Dehydrated ☐

TIDES

HIGH WATER :

LOW WATER :

SLACK WATER :

CURRENT ____ kn   DIRECTION ____ °

SEA CONDITIONS

SEA STATE

WATER TEMP

VISIBILITY

BEAUFORT SCALE

EQUIPMENT

Notes on additional equipment ...
_____
_____
_____
_____
_____

Skipper   Boat

Accumulated Dive Time To Date	Dive Time this Dive	Total Dive Time To Date
:	:	:

Verification Signature   Certification No.

Dive Record

Dive No _____ **Date** _____

Dive Site _____

AIR
| START psi/bar | − | END psi/bar | = | psi/bar | × | CYLINDER CAPACITY | = | AIR USED |

SURFACE AIR BREATHING RATE = _____ ltr per min

TIME
| SURFACE INTERVAL : | IN : | > | OUT : | = | DIVE DURATION | × | ABSOLUTE PRESSURE |

DECO - DEPTH

DECOMPRESSION / SAFETY STOPS

_____ mins at _____ m/ft _____ %

_____ mins at _____ m/ft _____ %

_____ mins at _____ m/ft _____ %

PRE DIVE GROUP | **MAX DEPTH** | **END DIVE GROUP**

Safety Margin: None 5% 10% 15% 20%

Computer / Decompression Tables Used: _____

WEIGHT

Weight Belt: _____ Kg/lbs

Integral BCD: _____ Kg/lbs

Ankle Weights: _____ Kg/lbs

Buoyancy: NEG - OK - POS

EXPOSURE

Suit: _____

Undersuit _____

Gloves _____

Hood _____

Assessment: COLD OK HOT

DCI RISK

Was this dive...
- Cold Water Dive ☐
- Decompression Dive ☐
- Deep Dive ☐
- Excessive Work ☐
- Missed Deco. Stops ☐
- Rapid Ascent ☐

Are you...
- Dehydrated ☐

TIDES

HIGH WATER : _____

LOW WATER : _____

SLACK WATER : _____

CURRENT _____ kn   DIRECTION _____ °

SEA CONDITIONS

SEA STATE

WATER TEMP

VISIBILITY

BEAUFORT SCALE

EQUIPMENT

Notes on additional equipment ...

_____

_____

_____

_____

_____

Skipper _____ **Boat** _____

Accumulated Dive Time To Date	Dive Time this Dive	Total Dive Time To Date
:	:	:

Verification Signature   **Certification No.**

Dive Record

Dive No | Date

Dive Site

AIR

START psi/bar − END psi/bar = psi/bar × CYLINDER CAPACITY = AIR USED

SURFACE AIR BREATHING RATE = ltr per min

TIME

SURFACE INTERVAL : | IN : | OUT : | DIVE DURATION = | × ABSOLUTE PRESSURE

DECO - DEPTH

DECOMPRESSION / SAFETY STOPS

_____ mins at _____ m/ft _____ %
_____ mins at _____ m/ft _____ %
_____ mins at _____ m/ft _____ %

PRE DIVE GROUP | MAX DEPTH | END DIVE GROUP

Safety Margin: None 5% 10% 15% 20%

Computer / Decompression Tables Used:

WEIGHT

Weight Belt: _____ Kg/lbs

Integral BCD: _____ Kg/lbs

Ankle Weights: _____ Kg/lbs

Buoyancy: NEG - OK - POS

EXPOSURE

Suit: _____

Undersuit _____

Gloves _____

Hood _____

Assessment: COLD OK HOT

DCI RISK

Was this dive...
Cold Water Dive ☐
Decompression Dive ☐
Deep Dive ☐
Excessive Work ☐
Missed Deco. Stops ☐
Rapid Ascent ☐
Are you...
Dehydrated ☐

TIDES

HIGH WATER :

LOW WATER :

SLACK WATER :

CURRENT _____ kn   DIRECTION _____ °

SEA CONDITIONS

SEA STATE

WATER TEMP

VISIBILITY

BEAUFORT SCALE

EQUIPMENT

Notes on additional equipment ...

Skipper | Boat

Accumulated Dive Time To Date	Dive Time this Dive	Total Dive Time To Date
:	:	:

Verification Signature   **Certification No.**

Dive Record

Dive No	Date

Dive Site

AIR
START psi/bar − END psi/bar = psi/bar × CYLINDER CAPACITY = AIR USED

SURFACE AIR BREATHING RATE = ltr per min

TIME
SURFACE INTERVAL : | IN : > OUT : = DIVE DURATION × ABSOLUTE PRESSURE

DECO - DEPTH

DECOMPRESSION / SAFETY STOPS
____ mins at ____ m/ft ____ %
____ mins at ____ m/ft ____ %
____ mins at ____ m/ft ____ %

PRE DIVE GROUP | MAX DEPTH | END DIVE GROUP

Safety Margin: None 5% 10% 15% 20%

Computer / Decompression Tables Used:

WEIGHT

Weight Belt: _____ Kg/lbs

Integral BCD: _____ Kg/lbs

Ankle Weights: _____ Kg/lbs

Buoyancy: NEG - OK - POS

EXPOSURE

Suit: _____
Undersuit _____
Gloves _____
Hood _____
Assessment: COLD OK HOT

DCI RISK

Was this dive...
Cold Water Dive ☐
Decompression Dive ☐
Deep Dive ☐
Excessive Work ☐
Missed Deco. Stops ☐
Rapid Ascent ☐
Are you...
Dehydrated ☐

TIDES

HIGH WATER :

LOW WATER :

SLACK WATER :

CURRENT _____ kn   DIRECTION _____ °

SEA CONDITIONS

SEA STATE

WATER TEMP

VISIBILITY

BEAUFORT SCALE

EQUIPMENT

Notes on additional equipment ...
_____
_____
_____
_____

Skipper	Boat

Accumulated Dive Time To Date	Dive Time this Dive	Total Dive Time To Date
:	:	:

Verification Signature   Certification No.

Dive Record

Dive No | **Date**

Dive Site

AIR
START psi/bar − END psi/bar = psi/bar × CYLINDER CAPACITY = AIR USED / ABSOLUTE PRESSURE = SURFACE AIR BREATHING RATE ltr per min

TIME
SURFACE INTERVAL : | IN : | > | OUT : | = DIVE DURATION | × ABSOLUTE PRESSURE

DECO - DEPTH
DECOMPRESSION / SAFETY STOPS
____ mins at ____ m/ft ____ %
____ mins at ____ m/ft ____ %
____ mins at ____ m/ft ____ %

PRE DIVE GROUP | MAX DEPTH | END DIVE GROUP

Safety Margin: None 5% 10% 15% 20%

Computer / Decompression Tables Used:

WEIGHT

Weight Belt: ____ Kg/lbs

Integral BCD: ____ Kg/lbs

Ankle Weights: ____ Kg/lbs

Buoyancy: NEG - OK - POS

EXPOSURE

Suit: ____
Undersuit ____
Gloves ____
Hood ____

Assessment: COLD OK HOT

DCI RISK

Was this dive...
Cold Water Dive ☐
Decompression Dive ☐
Deep Dive ☐
Excessive Work ☐
Missed Deco. Stops ☐
Rapid Ascent ☐
Are you...
Dehydrated ☐

TIDES

HIGH WATER :

LOW WATER :

SLACK WATER :

CURRENT ____ kn   DIRECTION ____ °

SEA CONDITIONS

SEA STATE

WATER TEMP

VISIBILITY

BEAUFORT SCALE

EQUIPMENT

Notes on additional equipment ...

Skipper | **Boat**

Accumulated Dive Time To Date	Dive Time this Dive	Total Dive Time To Date
:	:	:

Verification Signature   **Certification No.**

Dive Record

Dive No **Date**

Dive Site

AIR
| START psi/bar | − | END psi/bar | = | psi/bar | × | CYLINDER CAPACITY | = | AIR USED | SURFACE AIR BREATHING RATE |

= _____ ltr per min

TIME
| SURFACE INTERVAL : | IN : | > | OUT : | = | DIVE DURATION | × | ABSOLUTE PRESSURE |

DECO - DEPTH

DECOMPRESSION / SAFETY STOPS

_____ mins at _____ m/ft _____ %
_____ mins at _____ m/ft _____ %
_____ mins at _____ m/ft _____ %

PRE DIVE GROUP   MAX DEPTH   END DIVE GROUP

Safety Margin: None 5% 10% 15% 20%

Computer / Decompression Tables Used:

WEIGHT

Weight Belt: _____ Kg/lbs
Integral BCD: _____ Kg/lbs
Ankle Weights: _____ Kg/lbs
Buoyancy: NEG - OK - POS

EXPOSURE

Suit: _____
Undersuit _____
Gloves _____
Hood _____
Assessment: COLD OK HOT

DCI RISK

Was this dive...
Cold Water Dive ☐
Decompression Dive ☐
Deep Dive ☐
Excessive Work ☐
Missed Deco. Stops ☐
Rapid Ascent ☐
Are you...
Dehydrated ☐

TIDES

HIGH WATER   :
LOW WATER   :
SLACK WATER   :
CURRENT _____ kn   DIRECTION _____ °

SEA CONDITIONS

SEA STATE
WATER TEMP
VISIBILITY
BEAUFORT SCALE

EQUIPMENT

Notes on additional equipment ...

Skipper   **Boat**

Accumulated Dive Time To Date	Dive Time this Dive	Total Dive Time To Date
:	:	:

Verification Signature   **Certification No.**

Dive Record

Dive No

Date

Dive Site

AIR

| START psi/bar | − | END psi/bar | = | psi/bar | × | CYLINDER CAPACITY | = | AIR USED | / | SURFACE AIR BREATHING RATE = ltr per min |

TIME

| SURFACE INTERVAL : | | IN : | > | OUT : | = | DIVE DURATION | × | ABSOLUTE PRESSURE |

DECO - DEPTH

DECOMPRESSION / SAFETY STOPS

_____ mins at _____ m/ft _____ %
_____ mins at _____ m/ft _____ %
_____ mins at _____ m/ft _____ %

PRE DIVE GROUP

MAX DEPTH

END DIVE GROUP

Safety Margin: None 5% 10% 15% 20%

Computer / Decompression Tables Used:

WEIGHT

Weight Belt: _____ Kg/lbs

Integral BCD: _____ Kg/lbs

Ankle Weights: _____ Kg/lbs

Buoyancy: NEG - OK - POS

EXPOSURE

Suit: _____

Undersuit _____

Gloves _____

Hood _____

Assessment: COLD OK HOT

DCI RISK

Was this dive...
Cold Water Dive ☐
Decompression Dive ☐
Deep Dive ☐
Excessive Work ☐
Missed Deco. Stops ☐
Rapid Ascent ☐
Are you...
Dehydrated ☐

TIDES

HIGH WATER :

LOW WATER :

SLACK WATER :

CURRENT _____ kn   DIRECTION _____ °

SEA CONDITIONS

SEA STATE

WATER TEMP

VISIBILITY

BEAUFORT SCALE

EQUIPMENT

Notes on additional equipment ...
_____
_____
_____
_____
_____

Skipper   **Boat**

Accumulated Dive Time To Date	Dive Time this Dive	Total Dive Time To Date
:	:	:

Verification Signature   Certification No.

Dive Record

Dive No | **Date**

Dive Site

AIR
START psi/bar − END psi/bar = psi/bar × CYLINDER CAPACITY = AIR USED

SURFACE AIR BREATHING RATE = ltr per min

TIME
SURFACE INTERVAL : | IN : > OUT : = DIVE DURATION × ABSOLUTE PRESSURE

DECO - DEPTH
DECOMPRESSION / SAFETY STOPS
____ mins at ____ m/ft ____ %
____ mins at ____ m/ft ____ %
____ mins at ____ m/ft ____ %

PRE DIVE GROUP | MAX DEPTH | END DIVE GROUP

Safety Margin: None 5% 10% 15% 20%

Computer / Decompression Tables Used:

WEIGHT

Weight Belt: _____ Kg/lbs

Integral BCD: _____ Kg/lbs

Ankle Weights: _____ Kg/lbs

Buoyancy: NEG - OK - POS

EXPOSURE

Suit: _____

Undersuit _____

Gloves _____

Hood _____

Assessment: COLD OK HOT

DCI RISK

Was this dive...
Cold Water Dive ☐
Decompression Dive ☐
Deep Dive ☐
Excessive Work ☐
Missed Deco. Stops ☐
Rapid Ascent ☐
Are you...
Dehydrated ☐

TIDES

HIGH WATER :

LOW WATER :

SLACK WATER :

CURRENT ____ kn   DIRECTION ____ °

SEA CONDITIONS

SEA STATE

WATER TEMP

VISIBILITY

BEAUFORT SCALE

EQUIPMENT

Notes on additional equipment ...

Skipper | **Boat**

Accumulated Dive Time To Date	Dive Time this Dive	Total Dive Time To Date
:	:	:

Verification Signature   **Certification No.**

Dive Record

Dive No | **Date**

Dive Site

AIR

| START psi/bar | − | END psi/bar | = | psi/bar | × | CYLINDER CAPACITY | = | AIR USED | / | SURFACE AIR BREATHING RATE = ltr per min |

TIME

| SURFACE INTERVAL : | | IN : | > | OUT : | = | DIVE DURATION | × | ABSOLUTE PRESSURE |

DECO - DEPTH

DECOMPRESSION / SAFETY STOPS

_____ mins at _____ m/ft _____ %
_____ mins at _____ m/ft _____ %
_____ mins at _____ m/ft _____ %

PRE DIVE GROUP | MAX DEPTH | END DIVE GROUP

Safety Margin: None 5% 10% 15% 20%

Computer / Decompression Tables Used:

WEIGHT

Weight Belt: _____ Kg/lbs

Integral BCD: _____ Kg/lbs

Ankle Weights: _____ Kg/lbs

Buoyancy: NEG - OK - POS

EXPOSURE

Suit: _____

Undersuit _____

Gloves _____

Hood _____

Assessment: COLD OK HOT

DCI RISK

Was this dive...
Cold Water Dive ☐
Decompression Dive ☐
Deep Dive ☐
Excessive Work ☐
Missed Deco. Stops ☐
Rapid Ascent ☐
Are you...
Dehydrated ☐

TIDES

HIGH WATER :

LOW WATER :

SLACK WATER :

CURRENT _____ kn   DIRECTION _____ °

SEA CONDITIONS

SEA STATE

WATER TEMP

VISIBILITY

BEAUFORT SCALE

EQUIPMENT

Notes on additional equipment ...

Skipper | **Boat**

Accumulated Dive Time To Date	Dive Time this Dive	Total Dive Time To Date
:	:	:

Verification Signature Certification No.

Dive Record

Dive No **Date**

Dive Site

AIR: START psi/bar − END psi/bar = psi/bar × CYLINDER CAPACITY = AIR USED / SURFACE AIR BREATHING RATE = ltr per min

TIME: SURFACE INTERVAL : | IN : > OUT : = DIVE DURATION × ABSOLUTE PRESSURE

DECO - DEPTH:
DECOMPRESSION / SAFETY STOPS
____ mins at ____ m/ft ____ %
____ mins at ____ m/ft ____ %
____ mins at ____ m/ft ____ %

PRE DIVE GROUP | MAX DEPTH | END DIVE GROUP

Safety Margin: None 5% 10% 15% 20%

Computer / Decompression Tables Used:

WEIGHT

Weight Belt: _____ Kg/lbs
Integral BCD: _____ Kg/lbs
Ankle Weights: _____ Kg/lbs
Buoyancy: NEG - OK - POS

EXPOSURE

Suit: _____
Undersuit _____
Gloves _____
Hood _____
Assessment: COLD OK HOT

DCI RISK

Was this dive...
Cold Water Dive ☐
Decompression Dive ☐
Deep Dive ☐
Excessive Work ☐
Missed Deco. Stops ☐
Rapid Ascent ☐
Are you...
Dehydrated ☐

TIDES

HIGH WATER :
LOW WATER :
SLACK WATER :
CURRENT ____ kn   DIRECTION ____ °

SEA CONDITIONS

SEA STATE
WATER TEMP
VISIBILITY
BEAUFORT SCALE

EQUIPMENT

Notes on additional equipment ...

Skipper **Boat**

Accumulated Dive Time To Date	Dive Time this Dive	Total Dive Time To Date
:	:	:

Verification Signature   **Certification No.**

Dive Record

Dive No | **Date**

Dive Site

AIR
START psi/bar − END psi/bar = psi/bar × CYLINDER CAPACITY = AIR USED

SURFACE AIR BREATHING RATE = ltr per min

TIME
SURFACE INTERVAL : | IN : > OUT : = DIVE DURATION × ABSOLUTE PRESSURE

DECO - DEPTH
DECOMPRESSION / SAFETY STOPS
____ mins at ____ m/ft ____ %
____ mins at ____ m/ft ____ %
____ mins at ____ m/ft ____ %

PRE DIVE GROUP | MAX DEPTH | END DIVE GROUP

Safety Margin: None 5% 10% 15% 20%

Computer / Decompression Tables Used:

WEIGHT

Weight Belt: _____ Kg/lbs

Integral BCD: _____ Kg/lbs

Ankle Weights: _____ Kg/lbs

Buoyancy: NEG - OK - POS

EXPOSURE

Suit: _____

Undersuit _____

Gloves _____

Hood _____

Assessment: COLD OK HOT

DCI RISK

Was this dive...
Cold Water Dive ☐
Decompression Dive ☐
Deep Dive ☐
Excessive Work ☐
Missed Deco. Stops ☐
Rapid Ascent ☐
Are you...
Dehydrated ☐

TIDES

HIGH WATER :

LOW WATER :

SLACK WATER :

CURRENT ____ kn DIRECTION ____ °

SEA CONDITIONS

SEA STATE

WATER TEMP

VISIBILITY

BEAUFORT SCALE

EQUIPMENT

Notes on additional equipment ...

Skipper | Boat

Accumulated Dive Time To Date	Dive Time this Dive	Total Dive Time To Date
:	:	:

Verification Signature   **Certification No.**

Dive Record

Dive No: _____ **Date:** _____

Dive Site: _____

AIR

START psi/bar − END psi/bar = psi/bar × CYLINDER CAPACITY = AIR USED

SURFACE AIR BREATHING RATE = ____ ltr per min

TIME

SURFACE INTERVAL : ___   IN : ___ > OUT : ___ = DIVE DURATION × ABSOLUTE PRESSURE

DECO - DEPTH

DECOMPRESSION / SAFETY STOPS

_____ mins at _____ m/ft _____ %
_____ mins at _____ m/ft _____ %
_____ mins at _____ m/ft _____ %

PRE DIVE GROUP | MAX DEPTH | END DIVE GROUP

Safety Margin: None 5% 10% 15% 20%

Computer / Decompression Tables Used: _____

WEIGHT

Weight Belt: _____ Kg/lbs

Integral BCD: _____ Kg/lbs

Ankle Weights: _____ Kg/lbs

Buoyancy: NEG - OK - POS

EXPOSURE

Suit: _____

Undersuit _____

Gloves _____

Hood _____

Assessment: COLD OK HOT

DCI RISK

Was this dive...
Cold Water Dive ☐
Decompression Dive ☐
Deep Dive ☐
Excessive Work ☐
Missed Deco. Stops ☐
Rapid Ascent ☐
Are you...
Dehydrated ☐

TIDES

HIGH WATER : _____

LOW WATER : _____

SLACK WATER : _____

CURRENT _____ kn   DIRECTION _____ °

SEA CONDITIONS

SEA STATE _____

WATER TEMP _____

VISIBILITY _____

BEAUFORT SCALE _____

EQUIPMENT

Notes on additional equipment ...
_____
_____
_____
_____
_____

Skipper _____   **Boat** _____

Accumulated Dive Time To Date	Dive Time this Dive	Total Dive Time To Date
:	:	:

Verification Signature Certification No.

Dive Record

Dive No | **Date**

Dive Site

AIR: START psi/bar − END psi/bar = psi/bar × CYLINDER CAPACITY = AIR USED

SURFACE AIR BREATHING RATE = ltr per min

TIME: SURFACE INTERVAL : | IN : > OUT : = DIVE DURATION × ABSOLUTE PRESSURE

DECO - DEPTH:

DECOMPRESSION / SAFETY STOPS
_____ mins at _____ m/ft _____ %
_____ mins at _____ m/ft _____ %
_____ mins at _____ m/ft _____ %

PRE DIVE GROUP | MAX DEPTH | END DIVE GROUP

Safety Margin: None 5% 10% 15% 20%

Computer / Decompression Tables Used:

WEIGHT

Weight Belt: _____ Kg/lbs

Integral BCD: _____ Kg/lbs

Ankle Weights: _____ Kg/lbs

Buoyancy: NEG - OK - POS

EXPOSURE

Suit: _____

Undersuit _____

Gloves _____

Hood _____

Assessment: COLD OK HOT

DCI RISK

Was this dive...
Cold Water Dive ☐
Decompression Dive ☐
Deep Dive ☐
Excessive Work ☐
Missed Deco. Stops ☐
Rapid Ascent ☐
Are you...
Dehydrated ☐

TIDES

HIGH WATER :

LOW WATER :

SLACK WATER :

CURRENT _____ kn   DIRECTION _____ °

SEA CONDITIONS

SEA STATE

WATER TEMP

VISIBILITY

BEAUFORT SCALE

EQUIPMENT

Notes on additional equipment ...

Skipper | Boat

Accumulated Dive Time To Date	Dive Time this Dive	Total Dive Time To Date
:	:	:

Verification Signature   Certification No.

Dive Record

Dive No
Date
Dive Site

AIR

| START psi/bar | − | END psi/bar | = | psi/bar | × | CYLINDER CAPACITY | = | AIR USED | | SURFACE AIR BREATHING RATE |

= _____ ltr per min

TIME

| SURFACE INTERVAL | IN | > | OUT | = | DIVE DURATION | × | ABSOLUTE PRESSURE |

DECO - DEPTH

DECOMPRESSION / SAFETY STOPS
_____ mins at _____ m/ft _____ %
_____ mins at _____ m/ft _____ %
_____ mins at _____ m/ft _____ %

PRE DIVE GROUP | MAX DEPTH | END DIVE GROUP

Safety Margin: None 5% 10% 15% 20%

Computer / Decompression Tables Used:

WEIGHT

Weight Belt: _____ Kg/lbs
Integral BCD: _____ Kg/lbs
Ankle Weights: _____ Kg/lbs
Buoyancy: NEG - OK - POS

EXPOSURE

Suit: _____
Undersuit _____
Gloves _____
Hood _____
Assessment: COLD OK HOT

DCI RISK

Was this dive...
Cold Water Dive ☐
Decompression Dive ☐
Deep Dive ☐
Excessive Work ☐
Missed Deco. Stops ☐
Rapid Ascent ☐
Are you...
Dehydrated ☐

TIDES

HIGH WATER :
LOW WATER :
SLACK WATER :
CURRENT _____ kn   DIRECTION _____ °

SEA CONDITIONS

SEA STATE
WATER TEMP
VISIBILITY
BEAUFORT SCALE

EQUIPMENT

Notes on additional equipment ...

Skipper
Boat

Accumulated Dive Time To Date	Dive Time this Dive	Total Dive Time To Date
:	:	:

Verification Signature   **Certification No.**

Dive Record

Dive No | **Date**

Dive Site

AIR

START psi/bar − END psi/bar = psi/bar × CYLINDER CAPACITY = AIR USED

SURFACE AIR BREATHING RATE = ____ ltr per min

TIME

SURFACE INTERVAL : | IN : > OUT : = DIVE DURATION × ABSOLUTE PRESSURE

DECO - DEPTH

DECOMPRESSION / SAFETY STOPS

_____ mins at _____ m/ft _____ %

_____ mins at _____ m/ft _____ %

_____ mins at _____ m/ft _____ %

PRE DIVE GROUP | MAX DEPTH | END DIVE GROUP

Safety Margin: None 5% 10% 15% 20%

Computer / Decompression Tables Used:

WEIGHT

Weight Belt: _____ Kg/lbs

Integral BCD: _____ Kg/lbs

Ankle Weights: _____ Kg/lbs

Buoyancy: NEG - OK - POS

EXPOSURE

Suit: _____

Undersuit _____

Gloves _____

Hood _____

Assessment: COLD OK HOT

DCI RISK

Was this dive...
Cold Water Dive ☐
Decompression Dive ☐
Deep Dive ☐
Excessive Work ☐
Missed Deco. Stops ☐
Rapid Ascent ☐
Are you...
Dehydrated ☐

TIDES

HIGH WATER :

LOW WATER :

SLACK WATER :

CURRENT _____ kn   DIRECTION _____ °

SEA CONDITIONS

SEA STATE

WATER TEMP

VISIBILITY

BEAUFORT SCALE

EQUIPMENT

Notes on additional equipment ...

Skipper | **Boat**

Accumulated Dive Time To Date	Dive Time this Dive	Total Dive Time To Date
:	:	:

Verification Signature **Certification No.**

Dive Record

Dive No   **Date**

Dive Site

AIR

START psi/bar − END psi/bar = psi/bar × CYLINDER CAPACITY = AIR USED

SURFACE AIR BREATHING RATE

= ltr per min

TIME

SURFACE INTERVAL :   IN :   >   OUT :   = DIVE DURATION × ABSOLUTE PRESSURE

DECO - DEPTH

DECOMPRESSION / SAFETY STOPS

_____ mins at _____ m/ft _____ %

_____ mins at _____ m/ft _____ %

_____ mins at _____ m/ft _____ %

PRE DIVE GROUP   MAX DEPTH   END DIVE GROUP

Safety Margin: None   5%   10%   15%   20%

Computer / Decompression Tables Used:

WEIGHT

Weight Belt: _____ Kg/lbs

Integral BCD: _____ Kg/lbs

Ankle Weights: _____ Kg/lbs

Buoyancy: NEG - OK - POS

EXPOSURE

Suit: _____

Undersuit _____

Gloves _____

Hood _____

Assessment: COLD   OK   HOT

DCI RISK

Was this dive...
Cold Water Dive ☐
Decompression Dive ☐
Deep Dive ☐
Excessive Work ☐
Missed Deco. Stops ☐
Rapid Ascent ☐
Are you...
Dehydrated ☐

TIDES

HIGH WATER   :

LOW WATER   :

SLACK WATER   :

CURRENT _____ kn   DIRECTION _____ °

SEA CONDITIONS

SEA STATE

WATER TEMP

VISIBILITY

BEAUFORT SCALE

EQUIPMENT

Notes on additional equipment ...

Skipper   **Boat**

Accumulated Dive Time To Date	Dive Time this Dive	Total Dive Time To Date
:	:	:

Verification Signature · Certification No.

Dive Record

Dive No _____   Date _____

Dive Site _____

AIR
| START psi/bar | − | END psi/bar | = | psi/bar | × | CYLINDER CAPACITY | = | AIR USED |

SURFACE AIR BREATHING RATE = _____ ltr per min

TIME
| SURFACE INTERVAL : | IN : | > | OUT : | = | DIVE DURATION | × | ABSOLUTE PRESSURE |

DECO - DEPTH

DECOMPRESSION / SAFETY STOPS
_____ mins at _____ m/ft _____ %
_____ mins at _____ m/ft _____ %
_____ mins at _____ m/ft _____ %

PRE DIVE GROUP   MAX DEPTH   END DIVE GROUP

Safety Margin: None 5% 10% 15% 20%

Computer / Decompression Tables Used: _____

WEIGHT

Weight Belt: _____ Kg/lbs

Integral BCD: _____ Kg/lbs

Ankle Weights: _____ Kg/lbs

Buoyancy: NEG - OK - POS

EXPOSURE

Suit: _____

Undersuit _____

Gloves _____

Hood _____

Assessment: COLD OK HOT

DCI RISK

Was this dive...
Cold Water Dive ☐
Decompression Dive ☐
Deep Dive ☐
Excessive Work ☐
Missed Deco. Stops ☐
Rapid Ascent ☐
Are you...
Dehydrated ☐

TIDES

HIGH WATER : _____

LOW WATER : _____

SLACK WATER : _____

CURRENT _____ kn   DIRECTION _____ °

SEA CONDITIONS

SEA STATE _____

WATER TEMP _____

VISIBILITY _____

BEAUFORT SCALE _____

EQUIPMENT

Notes on additional equipment ...
_____
_____
_____
_____

Skipper _____   Boat _____

Accumulated Dive Time To Date	Dive Time this Dive	Total Dive Time To Date
:	:	:

Verification Signature   **Certification No.**

Dive Record

Dive No | **Date**

Dive Site

AIR
START psi/bar − END psi/bar = psi/bar × CYLINDER CAPACITY = AIR USED

SURFACE AIR BREATHING RATE = ltr per min

TIME
SURFACE INTERVAL : | IN : > OUT : = DIVE DURATION × ABSOLUTE PRESSURE

DECO - DEPTH
DECOMPRESSION / SAFETY STOPS

_____ mins at _____ m/ft _____ %

_____ mins at _____ m/ft _____ %

_____ mins at _____ m/ft _____ %

PRE DIVE GROUP | MAX DEPTH | END DIVE GROUP

Safety Margin: None 5% 10% 15% 20%

Computer / Decompression Tables Used:

WEIGHT

Weight Belt: _____ Kg/lbs

Integral BCD: _____ Kg/lbs

Ankle Weights: _____ Kg/lbs

Buoyancy: NEG - OK - POS

EXPOSURE

Suit: _____

Undersuit _____

Gloves _____

Hood _____

Assessment: COLD OK HOT

DCI RISK

Was this dive...
Cold Water Dive ☐
Decompression Dive ☐
Deep Dive ☐
Excessive Work ☐
Missed Deco. Stops ☐
Rapid Ascent ☐
Are you...
Dehydrated ☐

TIDES

HIGH WATER :

LOW WATER :

SLACK WATER :

CURRENT _____ kn   DIRECTION _____ °

SEA CONDITIONS

SEA STATE

WATER TEMP

VISIBILITY

BEAUFORT SCALE

EQUIPMENT

Notes on additional equipment ...

Skipper | Boat

Accumulated Dive Time To Date	Dive Time this Dive	Total Dive Time To Date
:	:	:

Verification Signature Certification No.

Dive Record

Dive No	Date

Dive Site

AIR: START psi/bar − END psi/bar = psi/bar × CYLINDER CAPACITY = AIR USED / ABSOLUTE PRESSURE = SURFACE AIR BREATHING RATE ltr per min

TIME: SURFACE INTERVAL : | IN : > OUT : = DIVE DURATION × ABSOLUTE PRESSURE

DECO - DEPTH:
DECOMPRESSION / SAFETY STOPS
____ mins at ____ m/ft ____ %
____ mins at ____ m/ft ____ %
____ mins at ____ m/ft ____ %

PRE DIVE GROUP | MAX DEPTH | END DIVE GROUP

Safety Margin: None 5% 10% 15% 20%

Computer / Decompression Tables Used:

WEIGHT

Weight Belt: ____ Kg/lbs
Integral BCD: ____ Kg/lbs
Ankle Weights: ____ Kg/lbs
Buoyancy: NEG - OK - POS

EXPOSURE

Suit: ____
Undersuit ____
Gloves ____
Hood ____
Assessment: COLD OK HOT

DCI RISK

Was this dive...
Cold Water Dive ☐
Decompression Dive ☐
Deep Dive ☐
Excessive Work ☐
Missed Deco. Stops ☐
Rapid Ascent ☐
Are you...
Dehydrated ☐

TIDES

HIGH WATER :
LOW WATER :
SLACK WATER :
CURRENT ____ kn   DIRECTION ____ °

SEA CONDITIONS

SEA STATE
WATER TEMP
VISIBILITY
BEAUFORT SCALE

EQUIPMENT

Notes on additional equipment ...

Skipper	Boat

Accumulated Dive Time To Date	Dive Time this Dive	Total Dive Time To Date
:	:	:

Verification Signature   Certification No.

Dive Record

Dive No | **Date**

Dive Site

AIR
START psi/bar − END psi/bar = psi/bar × CYLINDER CAPACITY = AIR USED

SURFACE AIR BREATHING RATE = ltr per min

TIME
SURFACE INTERVAL : | IN : > OUT : = DIVE DURATION × ABSOLUTE PRESSURE

DECO - DEPTH
DECOMPRESSION / SAFETY STOPS

_____ mins at _____ m/ft _____ %

_____ mins at _____ m/ft _____ %

_____ mins at _____ m/ft _____ %

PRE DIVE GROUP | MAX DEPTH | END DIVE GROUP

Safety Margin: None 5% 10% 15% 20%

Computer / Decompression Tables Used:

WEIGHT

Weight Belt:_____ Kg/lbs

Integral BCD:_____ Kg/lbs

Ankle Weights:_____ Kg/lbs

Buoyancy: NEG - OK - POS

EXPOSURE

Suit:_____

Undersuit_____

Gloves_____

Hood_____

Assessment: COLD OK HOT

DCI RISK

Was this dive...
Cold Water Dive ☐
Decompression Dive ☐
Deep Dive ☐
Excessive Work ☐
Missed Deco. Stops ☐
Rapid Ascent ☐
Are you...
Dehydrated ☐

TIDES

HIGH WATER :

LOW WATER :

SLACK WATER :

CURRENT _____ kn   DIRECTION _____ °

SEA CONDITIONS

SEA STATE

WATER TEMP

VISIBILITY

BEAUFORT SCALE

EQUIPMENT

Notes on additional equipment ...

Skipper | **Boat**

Accumulated Dive Time To Date	Dive Time this Dive	Total Dive Time To Date
:	:	:

Verification Signature **Certification No.**

Dive Record

Dive No | **Date**

Dive Site

AIR: START psi/bar − END psi/bar = psi/bar × CYLINDER CAPACITY = AIR USED / SURFACE AIR BREATHING RATE = ltr per min

TIME: SURFACE INTERVAL : | IN : > OUT : = DIVE DURATION × ABSOLUTE PRESSURE

DECO - DEPTH:

DECOMPRESSION / SAFETY STOPS
_____ mins at _____ m/ft _____ %
_____ mins at _____ m/ft _____ %
_____ mins at _____ m/ft _____ %

PRE DIVE GROUP | MAX DEPTH | END DIVE GROUP

Safety Margin: None 5% 10% 15% 20%

Computer / Decompression Tables Used:

WEIGHT

Weight Belt: _____ Kg/lbs

Integral BCD: _____ Kg/lbs

Ankle Weights: _____ Kg/lbs

Buoyancy: NEG - OK - POS

EXPOSURE

Suit: _____

Undersuit _____

Gloves _____

Hood _____

Assessment: COLD OK HOT

DCI RISK

Was this dive...
Cold Water Dive ☐
Decompression Dive ☐
Deep Dive ☐
Excessive Work ☐
Missed Deco. Stops ☐
Rapid Ascent ☐
Are you...
Dehydrated ☐

TIDES

HIGH WATER :

LOW WATER :

SLACK WATER :

CURRENT _____ kn   DIRECTION _____ °

SEA CONDITIONS

SEA STATE

WATER TEMP

VISIBILITY

BEAUFORT SCALE

EQUIPMENT

Notes on additional equipment ...

Skipper | **Boat**

Accumulated Dive Time To Date	Dive Time this Dive	Total Dive Time To Date
:	:	:

Verification Signature   **Certification No.**

Dive Record

Dive No **Date**

Dive Site

AIR
| START psi/bar | − | END psi/bar | = | psi/bar | × | CYLINDER CAPACITY | = | AIR USED | SURFACE AIR BREATHING RATE |

= ltr per min

TIME
| SURFACE INTERVAL : | IN : | > | OUT : | = | DIVE DURATION | × | ABSOLUTE PRESSURE |

DECO - DEPTH

DECOMPRESSION / SAFETY STOPS

____ mins at ____ m/ft ____ %
____ mins at ____ m/ft ____ %
____ mins at ____ m/ft ____ %

PRE DIVE GROUP | MAX DEPTH | END DIVE GROUP

Safety Margin: None 5% 10% 15% 20%

Computer / Decompression Tables Used:

WEIGHT

Weight Belt: _____ Kg/lbs
Integral BCD: _____ Kg/lbs
Ankle Weights: _____ Kg/lbs
Buoyancy: NEG - OK - POS

EXPOSURE

Suit: _____
Undersuit _____
Gloves _____
Hood _____
Assessment: COLD OK HOT

DCI RISK

Was this dive...
Cold Water Dive ☐
Decompression Dive ☐
Deep Dive ☐
Excessive Work ☐
Missed Deco. Stops ☐
Rapid Ascent ☐
Are you...
Dehydrated ☐

TIDES

HIGH WATER :
LOW WATER :
SLACK WATER :
CURRENT ____ kn DIRECTION ____ °

SEA CONDITIONS

SEA STATE
WATER TEMP
VISIBILITY
BEAUFORT SCALE

EQUIPMENT

Notes on additional equipment ...

Skipper **Boat**

Accumulated Dive Time To Date	Dive Time this Dive	Total Dive Time To Date
:	:	:

Verification Signature **Certification No.**

Dive Record

Dive No **Date**

Dive Site

AIR
| START psi/bar | − | END psi/bar | = | psi/bar | × | CYLINDER CAPACITY | = | AIR USED |

SURFACE AIR BREATHING RATE

= ltr per min

TIME
| SURFACE INTERVAL : | | IN : | > | OUT : | = | DIVE DURATION | × | ABSOLUTE PRESSURE |

DECO - DEPTH

DECOMPRESSION / SAFETY STOPS
_____ mins at _____ m/ft _____ %
_____ mins at _____ m/ft _____ %
_____ mins at _____ m/ft _____ %

PRE DIVE GROUP   MAX DEPTH   END DIVE GROUP

Safety Margin: None 5% 10% 15% 20%

Computer / Decompression Tables Used:

WEIGHT

Weight Belt: _____ Kg/lbs

Integral BCD: _____ Kg/lbs

Ankle Weights: _____ Kg/lbs

Buoyancy: NEG - OK - POS

EXPOSURE

Suit: _____
Undersuit _____
Gloves _____
Hood _____
Assessment: COLD OK HOT

DCI RISK

Was this dive...
Cold Water Dive ☐
Decompression Dive ☐
Deep Dive ☐
Excessive Work ☐
Missed Deco. Stops ☐
Rapid Ascent ☐
Are you...
Dehydrated ☐

TIDES

HIGH WATER :

LOW WATER :

SLACK WATER :

CURRENT _____ kn   DIRECTION _____ °

SEA CONDITIONS

SEA STATE

WATER TEMP

VISIBILITY

BEAUFORT SCALE

EQUIPMENT

Notes on additional equipment ...

Skipper   **Boat**

Accumulated Dive Time To Date	Dive Time this Dive	Total Dive Time To Date
:	:	:

Verification Signature Certification No.

Dive Record

Dive No | **Date**

Dive Site

AIR
START psi/bar − END psi/bar = psi/bar × CYLINDER CAPACITY = AIR USED

SURFACE AIR BREATHING RATE = ltr per min

TIME
SURFACE INTERVAL : | IN : > OUT : = DIVE DURATION × ABSOLUTE PRESSURE

DECO - DEPTH

DECOMPRESSION / SAFETY STOPS

_____ mins at _____ m/ft _____ %

_____ mins at _____ m/ft _____ %

_____ mins at _____ m/ft _____ %

PRE DIVE GROUP | MAX DEPTH | END DIVE GROUP

Safety Margin: None 5% 10% 15% 20%

Computer / Decompression Tables Used:

WEIGHT

Weight Belt: _____ Kg/lbs

Integral BCD: _____ Kg/lbs

Ankle Weights: _____ Kg/lbs

Buoyancy: NEG - OK - POS

EXPOSURE

Suit: _____

Undersuit _____

Gloves _____

Hood _____

Assessment: COLD OK HOT

DCI RISK

Was this dive...
Cold Water Dive ☐
Decompression Dive ☐
Deep Dive ☐
Excessive Work ☐
Missed Deco. Stops ☐
Rapid Ascent ☐
Are you...
Dehydrated ☐

TIDES

HIGH WATER :

LOW WATER :

SLACK WATER :

CURRENT _____ kn   DIRECTION _____ °

SEA CONDITIONS

SEA STATE

WATER TEMP

VISIBILITY

BEAUFORT SCALE

EQUIPMENT

Notes on additional equipment ...

Skipper | **Boat**

Accumulated Dive Time To Date	Dive Time this Dive	Total Dive Time To Date
:	:	:

Verification Signature Certification No.

Dive Record

Dive No | Date

Dive Site

AIR
START psi/bar − END psi/bar = psi/bar × CYLINDER CAPACITY = AIR USED

SURFACE AIR BREATHING RATE = ltr per min

TIME
SURFACE INTERVAL : | IN : > OUT : = DIVE DURATION × ABSOLUTE PRESSURE

DECO - DEPTH
DECOMPRESSION / SAFETY STOPS

_____ mins at _____ m/ft _____ %

_____ mins at _____ m/ft _____ %

_____ mins at _____ m/ft _____ %

PRE DIVE GROUP | MAX DEPTH | END DIVE GROUP

Safety Margin: None 5% 10% 15% 20%

Computer / Decompression Tables Used:

WEIGHT

Weight Belt: _____ Kg/lbs

Integral BCD: _____ Kg/lbs

Ankle Weights: _____ Kg/lbs

Buoyancy: NEG - OK - POS

EXPOSURE

Suit: _____

Undersuit _____

Gloves _____

Hood _____

Assessment: COLD OK HOT

DCI RISK

Was this dive...
Cold Water Dive ☐
Decompression Dive ☐
Deep Dive ☐
Excessive Work ☐
Missed Deco. Stops ☐
Rapid Ascent ☐
Are you...
Dehydrated ☐

TIDES

HIGH WATER :

LOW WATER :

SLACK WATER :

CURRENT _____ kn   DIRECTION _____ °

SEA CONDITIONS

SEA STATE

WATER TEMP

VISIBILITY

BEAUFORT SCALE

EQUIPMENT

Notes on additional equipment ...

Skipper | Boat

Accumulated Dive Time To Date	Dive Time this Dive	Total Dive Time To Date
:	:	:

Verification Signature **Certification No.**

Dive Record

Dive No | **Date**

Dive Site

AIR: START psi/bar − END psi/bar = psi/bar × CYLINDER CAPACITY = AIR USED / ABSOLUTE PRESSURE = SURFACE AIR BREATHING RATE ltr per min

TIME: SURFACE INTERVAL : | IN : > OUT : = DIVE DURATION × ABSOLUTE PRESSURE

DECO - DEPTH:
DECOMPRESSION / SAFETY STOPS
_____ mins at _____ m/ft _____ %
_____ mins at _____ m/ft _____ %
_____ mins at _____ m/ft _____ %

PRE DIVE GROUP | MAX DEPTH | END DIVE GROUP

Safety Margin: None 5% 10% 15% 20%

Computer / Decompression Tables Used:

WEIGHT

Weight Belt: _____ Kg/lbs

Integral BCD: _____ Kg/lbs

Ankle Weights: _____ Kg/lbs

Buoyancy: NEG - OK - POS

EXPOSURE

Suit: _____
Undersuit _____
Gloves _____
Hood _____
Assessment: COLD OK HOT

DCI RISK

Was this dive...
Cold Water Dive ☐
Decompression Dive ☐
Deep Dive ☐
Excessive Work ☐
Missed Deco. Stops ☐
Rapid Ascent ☐
Are you...
Dehydrated ☐

TIDES

HIGH WATER :
LOW WATER :
SLACK WATER :
CURRENT _____ kn   DIRECTION _____ °

SEA CONDITIONS

SEA STATE
WATER TEMP
VISIBILITY
BEAUFORT SCALE

EQUIPMENT

Notes on additional equipment ...

Skipper | **Boat**

Accumulated Dive Time To Date	Dive Time this Dive	Total Dive Time To Date
:	:	:

Verification Signature   Certification No.

Dive Record

Dive No | **Date**

Dive Site

AIR: START psi/bar − END psi/bar = psi/bar × CYLINDER CAPACITY = AIR USED / SURFACE AIR BREATHING RATE = ltr per min

TIME: SURFACE INTERVAL : | IN : | OUT : | = DIVE DURATION × ABSOLUTE PRESSURE

DECO - DEPTH:
DECOMPRESSION / SAFETY STOPS
___ mins at ___ m/ft ___ %
___ mins at ___ m/ft ___ %
___ mins at ___ m/ft ___ %

PRE DIVE GROUP | MAX DEPTH | END DIVE GROUP

Safety Margin: None 5% 10% 15% 20%

Computer / Decompression Tables Used:

WEIGHT

Weight Belt: ___ Kg/lbs
Integral BCD: ___ Kg/lbs
Ankle Weights: ___ Kg/lbs
Buoyancy: NEG - OK - POS

EXPOSURE

Suit: ___
Undersuit ___
Gloves ___
Hood ___
Assessment: COLD OK HOT

DCI RISK

Was this dive...
Cold Water Dive ☐
Decompression Dive ☐
Deep Dive ☐
Excessive Work ☐
Missed Deco. Stops ☐
Rapid Ascent ☐
Are you...
Dehydrated ☐

TIDES

HIGH WATER :
LOW WATER :
SLACK WATER :
CURRENT ___ kn DIRECTION ___ °

SEA CONDITIONS

SEA STATE
WATER TEMP
VISIBILITY
BEAUFORT SCALE

EQUIPMENT

Notes on additional equipment ...

Skipper | **Boat**

Accumulated Dive Time To Date	Dive Time this Dive	Total Dive Time To Date
:	:	:

Verification Signature   Certification No.

Dive Record

Dive No | **Date**

Dive Site

AIR

START psi/bar − END psi/bar = psi/bar × CYLINDER CAPACITY = AIR USED

SURFACE AIR BREATHING RATE = ltr per min

TIME

SURFACE INTERVAL : | IN : | OUT : | DIVE DURATION = | ABSOLUTE PRESSURE ×

DECO - DEPTH

DECOMPRESSION / SAFETY STOPS

_____ mins at _____ m/ft _____ %
_____ mins at _____ m/ft _____ %
_____ mins at _____ m/ft _____ %

PRE DIVE GROUP | MAX DEPTH | END DIVE GROUP

Safety Margin: None 5% 10% 15% 20%

Computer / Decompression Tables Used:

WEIGHT

Weight Belt: _____ Kg/lbs

Integral BCD: _____ Kg/lbs

Ankle Weights: _____ Kg/lbs

Buoyancy: NEG - OK - POS

EXPOSURE

Suit: _____

Undersuit _____

Gloves _____

Hood _____

Assessment: COLD OK HOT

DCI RISK

Was this dive...
Cold Water Dive ☐
Decompression Dive ☐
Deep Dive ☐
Excessive Work ☐
Missed Deco. Stops ☐
Rapid Ascent ☐
Are you...
Dehydrated ☐

TIDES

HIGH WATER :

LOW WATER :

SLACK WATER :

CURRENT _____ kn   DIRECTION _____ °

SEA CONDITIONS

SEA STATE

WATER TEMP

VISIBILITY

BEAUFORT SCALE

EQUIPMENT

Notes on additional equipment ...

_____
_____
_____
_____
_____

Skipper   **Boat**

Accumulated Dive Time To Date	Dive Time this Dive	Total Dive Time To Date
:	:	:

Verification Signature   **Certification No.**

Dive Record

Dive No | **Date**

Dive Site

AIR

START psi/bar − END psi/bar = psi/bar × CYLINDER CAPACITY = AIR USED

SURFACE AIR BREATHING RATE = ltr per min

TIME

SURFACE INTERVAL : | IN : > OUT : = DIVE DURATION × ABSOLUTE PRESSURE

DECO - DEPTH

DECOMPRESSION / SAFETY STOPS

_____ mins at _____ m/ft _____ %

_____ mins at _____ m/ft _____ %

_____ mins at _____ m/ft _____ %

PRE DIVE GROUP | MAX DEPTH | END DIVE GROUP

Safety Margin: None 5% 10% 15% 20%

Computer / Decompression Tables Used:

WEIGHT

Weight Belt: _____ Kg/lbs

Integral BCD: _____ Kg/lbs

Ankle Weights: _____ Kg/lbs

Buoyancy: NEG - OK - POS

EXPOSURE

Suit: _____

Undersuit _____

Gloves _____

Hood _____

Assessment: COLD OK HOT

DCI RISK

Was this dive...
Cold Water Dive ☐
Decompression Dive ☐
Deep Dive ☐
Excessive Work ☐
Missed Deco. Stops ☐
Rapid Ascent ☐
Are you...
Dehydrated ☐

TIDES

HIGH WATER :

LOW WATER :

SLACK WATER :

CURRENT _____ kn DIRECTION _____ °

SEA CONDITIONS

SEA STATE

WATER TEMP

VISIBILITY

BEAUFORT SCALE

EQUIPMENT

Notes on additional equipment ...

Skipper | **Boat**

Accumulated Dive Time To Date	Dive Time this Dive	Total Dive Time To Date
:	:	:

Verification Signature   **Certification No.**

Dive Record

Dive No:
Date:
Dive Site:

AIR
START psi/bar − END psi/bar = psi/bar × CYLINDER CAPACITY = AIR USED

SURFACE AIR BREATHING RATE = ltr per min

TIME
SURFACE INTERVAL : | IN : | OUT : | = DIVE DURATION × ABSOLUTE PRESSURE

DECO - DEPTH
DECOMPRESSION / SAFETY STOPS
_____ mins at _____ m/ft _____ %
_____ mins at _____ m/ft _____ %
_____ mins at _____ m/ft _____ %

PRE DIVE GROUP | MAX DEPTH | END DIVE GROUP

Safety Margin: None 5% 10% 15% 20%

Computer / Decompression Tables Used:

WEIGHT
Weight Belt: _____ Kg/lbs
Integral BCD: _____ Kg/lbs
Ankle Weights: _____ Kg/lbs
Buoyancy: NEG - OK - POS

EXPOSURE
Suit: _____
Undersuit _____
Gloves _____
Hood _____
Assessment: COLD OK HOT

DCI RISK
Was this dive...
Cold Water Dive ☐
Decompression Dive ☐
Deep Dive ☐
Excessive Work ☐
Missed Deco. Stops ☐
Rapid Ascent ☐
Are you...
Dehydrated ☐

TIDES
HIGH WATER :
LOW WATER :
SLACK WATER :
CURRENT _____ kn   DIRECTION _____ °

SEA CONDITIONS
SEA STATE
WATER TEMP
VISIBILITY
BEAUFORT SCALE

EQUIPMENT
Notes on additional equipment ...

Skipper   **Boat**

Accumulated Dive Time To Date	Dive Time this Dive	Total Dive Time To Date
:	:	:

Verification Signature   **Certification No.**

Dive Record

Dive No **Date**

Dive Site

AIR
START psi/bar − END psi/bar = psi/bar × CYLINDER CAPACITY = AIR USED

SURFACE AIR BREATHING RATE = ltr per min

TIME
SURFACE INTERVAL : | IN : > OUT : = DIVE DURATION × ABSOLUTE PRESSURE

DECO - DEPTH
DECOMPRESSION / SAFETY STOPS
_____ mins at _____ m/ft _____ %
_____ mins at _____ m/ft _____ %
_____ mins at _____ m/ft _____ %

PRE DIVE GROUP | MAX DEPTH | END DIVE GROUP

Safety Margin: None 5% 10% 15% 20%

Computer / Decompression Tables Used:

WEIGHT

Weight Belt: _____ Kg/lbs

Integral BCD: _____ Kg/lbs

Ankle Weights: _____ Kg/lbs

Buoyancy: NEG - OK - POS

EXPOSURE

Suit: _____

Undersuit _____

Gloves _____

Hood _____

Assessment: COLD OK HOT

DCI RISK

Was this dive...
Cold Water Dive ☐
Decompression Dive ☐
Deep Dive ☐
Excessive Work ☐
Missed Deco. Stops ☐
Rapid Ascent ☐
Are you...
Dehydrated ☐

TIDES

HIGH WATER :

LOW WATER :

SLACK WATER :

CURRENT _____ kn   DIRECTION _____ °

SEA CONDITIONS

SEA STATE

WATER TEMP

VISIBILITY

BEAUFORT SCALE

EQUIPMENT

Notes on additional equipment ...
_____
_____
_____
_____

Skipper   **Boat**

Accumulated Dive Time To Date	Dive Time this Dive	Total Dive Time To Date
:	:	:

Verification Signature   Certification No.

Dive Record

Dive No | **Date**

Dive Site

AIR

| START psi/bar | − | END psi/bar | = | psi/bar | × | CYLINDER CAPACITY | = | AIR USED | | SURFACE AIR BREATHING RATE |

= ltr per min

TIME

| SURFACE INTERVAL : | | IN : | > | OUT : | = | DIVE DURATION | × | ABSOLUTE PRESSURE |

DECO - DEPTH

DECOMPRESSION / SAFETY STOPS

_____ mins at _____ m/ft _____ %

_____ mins at _____ m/ft _____ %

_____ mins at _____ m/ft _____ %

| PRE DIVE GROUP | MAX DEPTH | END DIVE GROUP |

Safety Margin: None 5% 10% 15% 20%

Computer / Decompression Tables Used:

WEIGHT

Weight Belt: _____ Kg/lbs

Integral BCD: _____ Kg/lbs

Ankle Weights: _____ Kg/lbs

Buoyancy: NEG - OK - POS

EXPOSURE

Suit: _____

Undersuit _____

Gloves _____

Hood _____

Assessment: COLD OK HOT

DCI RISK

Was this dive...
Cold Water Dive ☐
Decompression Dive ☐
Deep Dive ☐
Excessive Work ☐
Missed Deco. Stops ☐
Rapid Ascent ☐
Are you...
Dehydrated ☐

TIDES

HIGH WATER :

LOW WATER :

SLACK WATER :

CURRENT _____ kn   DIRECTION _____ °

SEA CONDITIONS

SEA STATE

WATER TEMP

VISIBILITY

BEAUFORT SCALE

EQUIPMENT

Notes on additional equipment ...

Skipper | **Boat**

Accumulated Dive Time To Date	Dive Time this Dive	Total Dive Time To Date
:	:	:

Verification Signature   **Certification No.**

Dive Record

Dive No | **Date**

Dive Site

AIR
START psi/bar − END psi/bar = psi/bar × CYLINDER CAPACITY = AIR USED

SURFACE AIR BREATHING RATE = ltr per min

TIME
SURFACE INTERVAL : | IN : > OUT : = DIVE DURATION × ABSOLUTE PRESSURE

DECO - DEPTH
DECOMPRESSION / SAFETY STOPS
____mins at ____m/ft ____%
____mins at ____m/ft ____%
____mins at ____m/ft ____%

PRE DIVE GROUP | MAX DEPTH | END DIVE GROUP

Safety Margin: None 5% 10% 15% 20%

Computer / Decompression Tables Used:

WEIGHT

Weight Belt: ____Kg/lbs

Integral BCD: ____Kg/lbs

Ankle Weights: ____Kg/lbs

Buoyancy: NEG - OK - POS

EXPOSURE

Suit: ____

Undersuit ____

Gloves ____

Hood ____

Assessment: COLD OK HOT

DCI RISK

Was this dive...
Cold Water Dive ☐
Decompression Dive ☐
Deep Dive ☐
Excessive Work ☐
Missed Deco. Stops ☐
Rapid Ascent ☐
Are you...
Dehydrated ☐

TIDES

HIGH WATER :

LOW WATER :

SLACK WATER :

CURRENT ____kn   DIRECTION ____°

SEA CONDITIONS

SEA STATE

WATER TEMP

VISIBILITY

BEAUFORT SCALE

EQUIPMENT

Notes on additional equipment ...

Skipper | **Boat**

Accumulated Dive Time To Date	Dive Time this Dive	Total Dive Time To Date
:	:	:

Verification Signature　　　　　　　Certification No.

Dive Record

Dive No	Date

Dive Site

AIR: START psi/bar − END psi/bar = psi/bar × CYLINDER CAPACITY = AIR USED

SURFACE AIR BREATHING RATE = ltr per min

TIME: SURFACE INTERVAL : | IN : | OUT : | = DIVE DURATION × ABSOLUTE PRESSURE

DECO - DEPTH:

DECOMPRESSION / SAFETY STOPS
____ mins at ____ m/ft ____ %
____ mins at ____ m/ft ____ %
____ mins at ____ m/ft ____ %

PRE DIVE GROUP | MAX DEPTH | END DIVE GROUP

Safety Margin: None 5% 10% 15% 20%

Computer / Decompression Tables Used:

WEIGHT

Weight Belt: _____ Kg/lbs
Integral BCD: _____ Kg/lbs
Ankle Weights: _____ Kg/lbs
Buoyancy: NEG - OK - POS

EXPOSURE

Suit: _____
Undersuit _____
Gloves _____
Hood _____
Assessment: COLD OK HOT

DCI RISK

Was this dive...
Cold Water Dive ☐
Decompression Dive ☐
Deep Dive ☐
Excessive Work ☐
Missed Deco. Stops ☐
Rapid Ascent ☐
Are you...
Dehydrated ☐

TIDES

HIGH WATER :
LOW WATER :
SLACK WATER :
CURRENT ____ kn   DIRECTION ____ °

SEA CONDITIONS

SEA STATE
WATER TEMP
VISIBILITY
BEAUFORT SCALE

EQUIPMENT

Notes on additional equipment ...

Skipper	Boat

Accumulated Dive Time To Date	Dive Time this Dive	Total Dive Time To Date
:	:	:

Verification Signature   Certification No.

Dive Record

Dive No

Date

Dive Site

AIR

| START psi/bar | − | END psi/bar | = | psi/bar | × | CYLINDER CAPACITY | = | AIR USED |

SURFACE AIR BREATHING RATE

_____ ltr per min

TIME

| SURFACE INTERVAL : | | IN : | > | OUT : | = | DIVE DURATION | × | ABSOLUTE PRESSURE |

DECO - DEPTH

DECOMPRESSION / SAFETY STOPS

_____ mins at _____ m/ft _____ %

_____ mins at _____ m/ft _____ %

_____ mins at _____ m/ft _____ %

PRE DIVE GROUP

MAX DEPTH

END DIVE GROUP

Safety Margin: None 5% 10% 15% 20%

Computer / Decompression Tables Used:

WEIGHT

Weight Belt: _____ Kg/lbs

Integral BCD: _____ Kg/lbs

Ankle Weights: _____ Kg/lbs

Buoyancy: NEG - OK - POS

EXPOSURE

Suit: _____

Undersuit _____

Gloves _____

Hood _____

Assessment: COLD OK HOT

DCI RISK

Was this dive...
- Cold Water Dive ☐
- Decompression Dive ☐
- Deep Dive ☐
- Excessive Work ☐
- Missed Deco. Stops ☐
- Rapid Ascent ☐

Are you...
- Dehydrated ☐

TIDES

HIGH WATER :

LOW WATER :

SLACK WATER :

CURRENT _____ kn   DIRECTION _____ °

SEA CONDITIONS

SEA STATE

WATER TEMP

VISIBILITY

BEAUFORT SCALE

EQUIPMENT

Notes on additional equipment ...

Skipper

Boat

Accumulated Dive Time To Date	Dive Time this Dive	Total Dive Time To Date
:	:	:

Verification Signature　　　　　**Certification No.**

Dive Record

Dive No | **Date**

Dive Site

AIR
START psi/bar − END psi/bar = psi/bar × CYLINDER CAPACITY = AIR USED

SURFACE AIR BREATHING RATE = ltr per min

TIME
SURFACE INTERVAL : | IN : > OUT : = DIVE DURATION × ABSOLUTE PRESSURE

DECO - DEPTH
DECOMPRESSION / SAFETY STOPS

____ mins at ____ m/ft ____ %

____ mins at ____ m/ft ____ %

____ mins at ____ m/ft ____ %

PRE DIVE GROUP | MAX DEPTH | END DIVE GROUP

Safety Margin: None 5% 10% 15% 20%

Computer / Decompression Tables Used:

WEIGHT

Weight Belt: _____ Kg/lbs

Integral BCD: _____ Kg/lbs

Ankle Weights: _____ Kg/lbs

Buoyancy: NEG - OK - POS

EXPOSURE

Suit: _____

Undersuit _____

Gloves _____

Hood _____

Assessment: COLD OK HOT

DCI RISK

Was this dive...
Cold Water Dive ☐
Decompression Dive ☐
Deep Dive ☐
Excessive Work ☐
Missed Deco. Stops ☐
Rapid Ascent ☐
Are you...
Dehydrated ☐

TIDES

HIGH WATER :

LOW WATER :

SLACK WATER :

CURRENT ____ kn   DIRECTION ____ °

SEA CONDITIONS

SEA STATE

WATER TEMP

VISIBILITY

BEAUFORT SCALE

EQUIPMENT

Notes on additional equipment ...

_____

_____

_____

_____

Skipper | **Boat**

Accumulated Dive Time To Date	Dive Time this Dive	Total Dive Time To Date
:	:	:

Verification Signature   **Certification No.**

Dive Record

Dive No **Date**

Dive Site

AIR: START psi/bar − END psi/bar = psi/bar × CYLINDER CAPACITY = AIR USED

SURFACE AIR BREATHING RATE: ___ ltr per min

TIME: SURFACE INTERVAL : | IN : > OUT : = DIVE DURATION × ABSOLUTE PRESSURE

DECO - DEPTH

DECOMPRESSION / SAFETY STOPS
_____ mins at _____ m/ft _____ %
_____ mins at _____ m/ft _____ %
_____ mins at _____ m/ft _____ %

PRE DIVE GROUP | MAX DEPTH | END DIVE GROUP

Safety Margin: None 5% 10% 15% 20%

Computer / Decompression Tables Used:

WEIGHT

Weight Belt: _____ Kg/lbs

Integral BCD: _____ Kg/lbs

Ankle Weights: _____ Kg/lbs

Buoyancy: NEG - OK - POS

EXPOSURE

Suit: _____

Undersuit _____

Gloves _____

Hood _____

Assessment: COLD OK HOT

DCI RISK

Was this dive...
Cold Water Dive ☐
Decompression Dive ☐
Deep Dive ☐
Excessive Work ☐
Missed Deco. Stops ☐
Rapid Ascent ☐
Are you...
Dehydrated ☐

TIDES

HIGH WATER :

LOW WATER :

SLACK WATER :

CURRENT _____ kn   DIRECTION _____ °

SEA CONDITIONS

SEA STATE

WATER TEMP

VISIBILITY

BEAUFORT SCALE

EQUIPMENT

Notes on additional equipment ...

Skipper **Boat**

Accumulated Dive	Dive Time	Total Dive
Time To Date	this Dive	Time To Date
:	:	:

Verification Signature   Certification No.

Dive Record

Dive No | **Date**

Dive Site

AIR

| START psi/bar | – | END psi/bar | = | psi/bar | × | CYLINDER CAPACITY | = | AIR USED |

SURFACE AIR BREATHING RATE
= _____ ltr per min

TIME

| SURFACE INTERVAL : | IN : | > | OUT : | = | DIVE DURATION | × | ABSOLUTE PRESSURE |

DECO - DEPTH

DECOMPRESSION / SAFETY STOPS

_____ mins at _____ m/ft _____ %

_____ mins at _____ m/ft _____ %

_____ mins at _____ m/ft _____ %

PRE DIVE GROUP | MAX DEPTH | END DIVE GROUP

Safety Margin: None 5% 10% 15% 20%

Computer / Decompression Tables Used:

WEIGHT

Weight Belt: _____ Kg/lbs

Integral BCD: _____ Kg/lbs

Ankle Weights: _____ Kg/lbs

Buoyancy: NEG - OK - POS

EXPOSURE

Suit: _____

Undersuit _____

Gloves _____

Hood _____

Assessment: COLD OK HOT

DCI RISK

Was this dive...
Cold Water Dive ☐
Decompression Dive ☐
Deep Dive ☐
Excessive Work ☐
Missed Deco. Stops ☐
Rapid Ascent ☐
Are you...
Dehydrated ☐

TIDES

HIGH WATER :

LOW WATER :

SLACK WATER :

CURRENT _____ kn   DIRECTION _____ °

SEA CONDITIONS

SEA STATE

WATER TEMP

VISIBILITY

BEAUFORT SCALE

EQUIPMENT

Notes on additional equipment ...

_____
_____
_____
_____
_____

Skipper | **Boat**

Accumulated Dive Time To Date	Dive Time this Dive	Total Dive Time To Date
:	:	:

Verification Signature   Certification No.

Dive Record

Dive No

Date

Dive Site

AIR

START psi/bar − END psi/bar = psi/bar × CYLINDER CAPACITY = AIR USED

SURFACE AIR BREATHING RATE = ltr per min

TIME

SURFACE INTERVAL :

IN : > OUT : = DIVE DURATION × ABSOLUTE PRESSURE

DECO - DEPTH

DECOMPRESSION / SAFETY STOPS

_____ mins at _____ m/ft _____ %

_____ mins at _____ m/ft _____ %

_____ mins at _____ m/ft _____ %

PRE DIVE GROUP

MAX DEPTH

END DIVE GROUP

Safety Margin: None 5% 10% 15% 20%

Computer / Decompression Tables Used:

WEIGHT

Weight Belt: _____ Kg/lbs

Integral BCD: _____ Kg/lbs

Ankle Weights: _____ Kg/lbs

Buoyancy: NEG - OK - POS

EXPOSURE

Suit: _____

Undersuit _____

Gloves _____

Hood _____

Assessment: COLD OK HOT

DCI RISK

Was this dive...
Cold Water Dive ☐
Decompression Dive ☐
Deep Dive ☐
Excessive Work ☐
Missed Deco. Stops ☐
Rapid Ascent ☐
Are you...
Dehydrated ☐

TIDES

HIGH WATER :

LOW WATER :

SLACK WATER :

CURRENT _____ kn   DIRECTION _____ °

SEA CONDITIONS

SEA STATE

WATER TEMP

VISIBILITY

BEAUFORT SCALE

EQUIPMENT

Notes on additional equipment ...

Skipper   Boat

Accumulated Dive Time To Date	Dive Time this Dive	Total Dive Time To Date
:	:	:

Verification Signature　　　　　　　Certification No.

Dive Record

Dive No | **Date**

Dive Site

AIR
START psi/bar − END psi/bar = psi/bar × CYLINDER CAPACITY = AIR USED

SURFACE AIR BREATHING RATE = ltr per min

TIME
SURFACE INTERVAL : | IN : > OUT : = DIVE DURATION × ABSOLUTE PRESSURE

DECO - DEPTH
DECOMPRESSION / SAFETY STOPS

_____ mins at _____ m/ft _____ %

_____ mins at _____ m/ft _____ %

_____ mins at _____ m/ft _____ %

PRE DIVE GROUP | MAX DEPTH | END DIVE GROUP

Safety Margin: None 5% 10% 15% 20%

Computer / Decompression Tables Used:

WEIGHT

Weight Belt: _____ Kg/lbs

Integral BCD: _____ Kg/lbs

Ankle Weights: _____ Kg/lbs

Buoyancy: NEG - OK - POS

EXPOSURE

Suit: _____

Undersuit _____

Gloves _____

Hood _____

Assessment: COLD OK HOT

DCI RISK

Was this dive...
Cold Water Dive ☐
Decompression Dive ☐
Deep Dive ☐
Excessive Work ☐
Missed Deco. Stops ☐
Rapid Ascent ☐
Are you...
Dehydrated ☐

TIDES

HIGH WATER :

LOW WATER :

SLACK WATER :

CURRENT _____ kn   DIRECTION _____ °

SEA CONDITIONS

SEA STATE

WATER TEMP

VISIBILITY

BEAUFORT SCALE

EQUIPMENT

Notes on additional equipment ...

Skipper | **Boat**

Accumulated Dive Time To Date	Dive Time this Dive	Total Dive Time To Date
:	:	:

Verification Signature   Certification No.

Dive Record

Dive No **Date**

Dive Site

AIR

| START psi/bar | − | END psi/bar | = | psi/bar | × | CYLINDER CAPACITY | = | AIR USED |

SURFACE AIR BREATHING RATE: ____ ltr per min

TIME

| SURFACE INTERVAL : | | IN : | > | OUT : | = | DIVE DURATION | × | ABSOLUTE PRESSURE |

DECO - DEPTH

DECOMPRESSION / SAFETY STOPS
____ mins at ____ m/ft ____ %
____ mins at ____ m/ft ____ %
____ mins at ____ m/ft ____ %

PRE DIVE GROUP **MAX DEPTH** **END DIVE GROUP**

Safety Margin: None 5% 10% 15% 20%

Computer / Decompression Tables Used:

WEIGHT

Weight Belt: _____ Kg/lbs

Integral BCD: _____ Kg/lbs

Ankle Weights: _____ Kg/lbs

Buoyancy: NEG - OK - POS

EXPOSURE

Suit: _____

Undersuit _____

Gloves _____

Hood _____

Assessment: COLD OK HOT

DCI RISK

Was this dive...
Cold Water Dive ☐
Decompression Dive ☐
Deep Dive ☐
Excessive Work ☐
Missed Deco. Stops ☐
Rapid Ascent ☐
Are you...
Dehydrated ☐

TIDES

HIGH WATER :

LOW WATER :

SLACK WATER :

CURRENT ____ kn   DIRECTION ____ °

SEA CONDITIONS

SEA STATE

WATER TEMP

VISIBILITY

BEAUFORT SCALE

EQUIPMENT

Notes on additional equipment ...

Skipper **Boat**

Accumulated Dive Time To Date	Dive Time this Dive	Total Dive Time To Date
:	:	:

Verification Signature   **Certification No.**

Dive Record

Dive No | **Date**

Dive Site

AIR

START psi/bar − END psi/bar = psi/bar × CYLINDER CAPACITY = AIR USED

SURFACE AIR BREATHING RATE = ____ ltr per min

TIME

SURFACE INTERVAL : | IN : > OUT : = DIVE DURATION × ABSOLUTE PRESSURE

DECO - DEPTH

DECOMPRESSION / SAFETY STOPS
____mins at____m/ft____%
____mins at____m/ft____%
____mins at____m/ft____%

PRE DIVE GROUP | MAX DEPTH | END DIVE GROUP

Safety Margin: None 5% 10% 15% 20%

Computer / Decompression Tables Used:

WEIGHT

Weight Belt:____Kg/lbs

Integral BCD:____Kg/lbs

Ankle Weights:____Kg/lbs

Buoyancy: NEG - OK - POS

EXPOSURE

Suit:____
Undersuit____
Gloves____
Hood____
Assessment: COLD OK HOT

DCI RISK

Was this dive...
Cold Water Dive ☐
Decompression Dive ☐
Deep Dive ☐
Excessive Work ☐
Missed Deco. Stops ☐
Rapid Ascent ☐
Are you...
Dehydrated ☐

TIDES

HIGH WATER :

LOW WATER :

SLACK WATER :

CURRENT ____kn DIRECTION ____°

SEA CONDITIONS

SEA STATE

WATER TEMP

VISIBILITY

BEAUFORT SCALE

EQUIPMENT

Notes on additional equipment ...

Skipper | **Boat**

Accumulated Dive Time To Date	Dive Time this Dive	Total Dive Time To Date
:	:	:

Verification Signature   Certification No.

Dive Record

Dive No | **Date**

Dive Site

AIR
START psi/bar − END psi/bar = psi/bar × CYLINDER CAPACITY = AIR USED

SURFACE AIR BREATHING RATE = ltr per min

TIME
SURFACE INTERVAL : | IN : > OUT : = DIVE DURATION × ABSOLUTE PRESSURE

DECO - DEPTH
DECOMPRESSION / SAFETY STOPS
____ mins at ____ m/ft ____ %
____ mins at ____ m/ft ____ %
____ mins at ____ m/ft ____ %

PRE DIVE GROUP | MAX DEPTH | END DIVE GROUP

Safety Margin: None 5% 10% 15% 20%

Computer / Decompression Tables Used:

WEIGHT

Weight Belt: ____ Kg/lbs

Integral BCD: ____ Kg/lbs

Ankle Weights: ____ Kg/lbs

Buoyancy: NEG - OK - POS

EXPOSURE

Suit: ____

Undersuit ____

Gloves ____

Hood ____

Assessment: COLD OK HOT

DCI RISK

Was this dive...
Cold Water Dive ☐
Decompression Dive ☐
Deep Dive ☐
Excessive Work ☐
Missed Deco. Stops ☐
Rapid Ascent ☐
Are you...
Dehydrated ☐

TIDES

HIGH WATER :

LOW WATER :

SLACK WATER :

CURRENT ____ kn DIRECTION ____ °

SEA CONDITIONS

SEA STATE

WATER TEMP

VISIBILITY

BEAUFORT SCALE

EQUIPMENT

Notes on additional equipment ...
____
____
____
____
____

Skipper | **Boat**

Accumulated Dive Time To Date	Dive Time this Dive	Total Dive Time To Date
:	:	:

Verification Signature   Certification No.

Dive Record

Dive No | **Date**

Dive Site

AIR
START psi/bar − END psi/bar = psi/bar × CYLINDER CAPACITY = AIR USED

SURFACE AIR BREATHING RATE = ltr per min

TIME
SURFACE INTERVAL : | IN : > OUT : = DIVE DURATION × ABSOLUTE PRESSURE

DECO - DEPTH
DECOMPRESSION / SAFETY STOPS

_____ mins at _____ m/ft _____ %

_____ mins at _____ m/ft _____ %

_____ mins at _____ m/ft _____ %

PRE DIVE GROUP | MAX DEPTH | END DIVE GROUP

Safety Margin: None 5% 10% 15% 20%

Computer / Decompression Tables Used:

WEIGHT

Weight Belt: _____ Kg/lbs

Integral BCD: _____ Kg/lbs

Ankle Weights: _____ Kg/lbs

Buoyancy: NEG - OK - POS

EXPOSURE

Suit: _____

Undersuit _____

Gloves _____

Hood _____

Assessment: COLD OK HOT

DCI RISK

Was this dive...
Cold Water Dive ☐
Decompression Dive ☐
Deep Dive ☐
Excessive Work ☐
Missed Deco. Stops ☐
Rapid Ascent ☐
Are you...
Dehydrated ☐

TIDES

HIGH WATER :

LOW WATER :

SLACK WATER :

CURRENT _____ kn   DIRECTION _____ °

SEA CONDITIONS

SEA STATE

WATER TEMP

VISIBILITY

BEAUFORT SCALE

EQUIPMENT

Notes on additional equipment ...

_____
_____
_____
_____
_____

Skipper | **Boat**

Accumulated Dive Time To Date	Dive Time this Dive	Total Dive Time To Date
:	:	:

Verification Signature Certification No.

Dive Record

Dive No
Date
Dive Site

AIR
START psi/bar − END psi/bar = psi/bar × CYLINDER CAPACITY = AIR USED

SURFACE AIR BREATHING RATE = ltr per min

TIME
SURFACE INTERVAL : | IN : > OUT : = DIVE DURATION × ABSOLUTE PRESSURE

DECO - DEPTH
DECOMPRESSION / SAFETY STOPS

_____ mins at _____ m/ft _____ %

_____ mins at _____ m/ft _____ %

_____ mins at _____ m/ft _____ %

PRE DIVE GROUP | MAX DEPTH | END DIVE GROUP

Safety Margin: None 5% 10% 15% 20%

Computer / Decompression Tables Used:

WEIGHT

Weight Belt: _____ Kg/lbs

Integral BCD: _____ Kg/lbs

Ankle Weights: _____ Kg/lbs

Buoyancy: NEG - OK - POS

EXPOSURE

Suit: _____

Undersuit _____

Gloves _____

Hood _____

Assessment: COLD OK HOT

DCI RISK

Was this dive...
Cold Water Dive ☐
Decompression Dive ☐
Deep Dive ☐
Excessive Work ☐
Missed Deco. Stops ☐
Rapid Ascent ☐
Are you...
Dehydrated ☐

TIDES

HIGH WATER :

LOW WATER :

SLACK WATER :

CURRENT _____ kn   DIRECTION _____ °

SEA CONDITIONS

SEA STATE

WATER TEMP

VISIBILITY

BEAUFORT SCALE

EQUIPMENT

Notes on additional equipment ...

Skipper   **Boat**

Accumulated Dive Time To Date	Dive Time this Dive	Total Dive Time To Date
:	:	:

Verification Signature   **Certification No.**

Dive Record

Dive No | Date

Dive Site

AIR: START psi/bar − END psi/bar = psi/bar × CYLINDER CAPACITY = AIR USED / SURFACE AIR BREATHING RATE = ltr per min

TIME: SURFACE INTERVAL : | IN : > OUT : = DIVE DURATION × ABSOLUTE PRESSURE

DECO - DEPTH:
DECOMPRESSION / SAFETY STOPS
_____ mins at _____ m/ft _____ %
_____ mins at _____ m/ft _____ %
_____ mins at _____ m/ft _____ %

PRE DIVE GROUP | MAX DEPTH | END DIVE GROUP

Safety Margin: None 5% 10% 15% 20%

Computer / Decompression Tables Used:

WEIGHT

Weight Belt: _____ Kg/lbs

Integral BCD: _____ Kg/lbs

Ankle Weights: _____ Kg/lbs

Buoyancy: NEG - OK - POS

EXPOSURE

Suit: _____
Undersuit _____
Gloves _____
Hood _____
Assessment: COLD OK HOT

DCI RISK

Was this dive...
Cold Water Dive ☐
Decompression Dive ☐
Deep Dive ☐
Excessive Work ☐
Missed Deco. Stops ☐
Rapid Ascent ☐
Are you...
Dehydrated ☐

TIDES

HIGH WATER :

LOW WATER :

SLACK WATER :

CURRENT _____ kn   DIRECTION _____ °

SEA CONDITIONS

SEA STATE

WATER TEMP

VISIBILITY

BEAUFORT SCALE

EQUIPMENT

Notes on additional equipment ...

Skipper | Boat

Accumulated Dive Time To Date	Dive Time this Dive	Total Dive Time To Date
:	:	:

Verification Signature　　　　　　　　Certification No.

Dive Record

Dive No | **Date**

Dive Site

AIR

START psi/bar − END psi/bar = psi/bar × CYLINDER CAPACITY = AIR USED

SURFACE AIR BREATHING RATE = ltr per min

TIME

SURFACE INTERVAL : | IN : > OUT : = DIVE DURATION × ABSOLUTE PRESSURE

DECO - DEPTH

DECOMPRESSION / SAFETY STOPS

_____ mins at _____ m/ft _____ %

_____ mins at _____ m/ft _____ %

_____ mins at _____ m/ft _____ %

PRE DIVE GROUP | MAX DEPTH | END DIVE GROUP

Safety Margin: None 5% 10% 15% 20%

Computer / Decompression Tables Used:

WEIGHT

Weight Belt: _____ Kg/lbs

Integral BCD: _____ Kg/lbs

Ankle Weights: _____ Kg/lbs

Buoyancy: NEG - OK - POS

EXPOSURE

Suit: _____

Undersuit _____

Gloves _____

Hood _____

Assessment: COLD OK HOT

DCI RISK

Was this dive...
Cold Water Dive ☐
Decompression Dive ☐
Deep Dive ☐
Excessive Work ☐
Missed Deco. Stops ☐
Rapid Ascent ☐
Are you...
Dehydrated ☐

TIDES

HIGH WATER :

LOW WATER :

SLACK WATER :

CURRENT _____ kn DIRECTION _____ °

SEA CONDITIONS

SEA STATE

WATER TEMP

VISIBILITY

BEAUFORT SCALE

EQUIPMENT

Notes on additional equipment ...

_____

_____

_____

_____

Skipper | **Boat**

Accumulated Dive Time To Date	Dive Time this Dive	Total Dive Time To Date
:	:	:

Verification Signature　　　　　　Certification No.

Dive Record

Dive No | **Date**

Dive Site

AIR
START psi/bar − END psi/bar = psi/bar × CYLINDER CAPACITY = AIR USED

SURFACE AIR BREATHING RATE ____ ltr per min

TIME
SURFACE INTERVAL : | IN : > OUT : = DIVE DURATION × ABSOLUTE PRESSURE

DECO - DEPTH
DECOMPRESSION / SAFETY STOPS
____ mins at ____ m/ft ____ %
____ mins at ____ m/ft ____ %
____ mins at ____ m/ft ____ %

PRE DIVE GROUP | MAX DEPTH | END DIVE GROUP

Safety Margin: None 5% 10% 15% 20%

Computer / Decompression Tables Used:

WEIGHT

Weight Belt: _____ Kg/lbs

Integral BCD: _____ Kg/lbs

Ankle Weights: _____ Kg/lbs

Buoyancy: NEG - OK - POS

EXPOSURE

Suit: _____

Undersuit _____

Gloves _____

Hood _____

Assessment: COLD OK HOT

DCI RISK

Was this dive...
Cold Water Dive ☐
Decompression Dive ☐
Deep Dive ☐
Excessive Work ☐
Missed Deco. Stops ☐
Rapid Ascent ☐
Are you...
Dehydrated ☐

TIDES

HIGH WATER :

LOW WATER :

SLACK WATER :

CURRENT ____ kn   DIRECTION ____ °

SEA CONDITIONS

SEA STATE

WATER TEMP

VISIBILITY

BEAUFORT SCALE

EQUIPMENT

Notes on additional equipment ...
_____
_____
_____
_____

Skipper | **Boat**

Accumulated Dive Time To Date	Dive Time this Dive	Total Dive Time To Date
:	:	:

Verification Signature **Certification No.**

Dive Record

Dive No | **Date**

Dive Site

AIR

| START psi/bar | − | END psi/bar | = | psi/bar | × | CYLINDER CAPACITY | = | AIR USED |

SURFACE AIR BREATHING RATE = ____ ltr per min

TIME

| SURFACE INTERVAL : | IN : | > | OUT : | = | DIVE DURATION | × | ABSOLUTE PRESSURE |

DECO - DEPTH

DECOMPRESSION / SAFETY STOPS

____ mins at ____ m/ft ____ %
____ mins at ____ m/ft ____ %
____ mins at ____ m/ft ____ %

PRE DIVE GROUP | MAX DEPTH | END DIVE GROUP

Safety Margin: None 5% 10% 15% 20%

Computer / Decompression Tables Used:

WEIGHT

Weight Belt: ____ Kg/lbs

Integral BCD: ____ Kg/lbs

Ankle Weights: ____ Kg/lbs

Buoyancy: NEG - OK - POS

EXPOSURE

Suit: ____

Undersuit ____

Gloves ____

Hood ____

Assessment: COLD OK HOT

DCI RISK

Was this dive...
Cold Water Dive ☐
Decompression Dive ☐
Deep Dive ☐
Excessive Work ☐
Missed Deco. Stops ☐
Rapid Ascent ☐
Are you...
Dehydrated ☐

TIDES

HIGH WATER :

LOW WATER :

SLACK WATER :

CURRENT ____ kn   DIRECTION ____ °

SEA CONDITIONS

SEA STATE

WATER TEMP

VISIBILITY

BEAUFORT SCALE

EQUIPMENT

Notes on additional equipment ...

____
____
____
____

Skipper | **Boat**

Accumulated Dive Time To Date	Dive Time this Dive	Total Dive Time To Date
:	:	:

Verification Signature   Certification No.

Dive Record

Dive No **Date**

Dive Site

AIR

START psi/bar	−	END psi/bar	=	psi/bar	×	CYLINDER CAPACITY	=	AIR USED	SURFACE AIR BREATHING RATE

= ltr per min

TIME

| SURFACE INTERVAL : | | IN : | > | OUT : | = | DIVE DURATION | × | ABSOLUTE PRESSURE |

DECO - DEPTH

DECOMPRESSION / SAFETY STOPS

_____ mins at _____ m/ft _____ %

_____ mins at _____ m/ft _____ %

_____ mins at _____ m/ft _____ %

PRE DIVE GROUP   MAX DEPTH   END DIVE GROUP

Safety Margin: None 5% 10% 15% 20%

Computer / Decompression Tables Used:

WEIGHT

Weight Belt: _____ Kg/lbs

Integral BCD: _____ Kg/lbs

Ankle Weights: _____ Kg/lbs

Buoyancy: NEG - OK - POS

EXPOSURE

Suit: _____

Undersuit _____

Gloves _____

Hood _____

Assessment: COLD OK HOT

DCI RISK

Was this dive...
Cold Water Dive ☐
Decompression Dive ☐
Deep Dive ☐
Excessive Work ☐
Missed Deco. Stops ☐
Rapid Ascent ☐
Are you...
Dehydrated ☐

TIDES

HIGH WATER :

LOW WATER :

SLACK WATER :

CURRENT   DIRECTION
_____ kn   _____ °

SEA CONDITIONS

SEA STATE

WATER TEMP

VISIBILITY

BEAUFORT SCALE

EQUIPMENT

Notes on additional equipment ...

Skipper   **Boat**

Accumulated Dive Time To Date	Dive Time this Dive	Total Dive Time To Date
:	:	:

Verification Signature Certification No.

Dive Record

Dive No **Date**

Dive Site

AIR

| START psi/bar | − | END psi/bar | = | psi/bar | × | CYLINDER CAPACITY | = | AIR USED |

SURFACE AIR BREATHING RATE = ltr per min

TIME

| SURFACE INTERVAL : | | IN : | > | OUT : | = | DIVE DURATION | × | ABSOLUTE PRESSURE |

DECO - DEPTH

DECOMPRESSION / SAFETY STOPS

_____ mins at _____ m/ft _____ %

_____ mins at _____ m/ft _____ %

_____ mins at _____ m/ft _____ %

PRE DIVE GROUP | MAX DEPTH | END DIVE GROUP

Safety Margin: None 5% 10% 15% 20%

Computer / Decompression Tables Used:

WEIGHT

Weight Belt: _____ Kg/lbs

Integral BCD: _____ Kg/lbs

Ankle Weights: _____ Kg/lbs

Buoyancy: NEG - OK - POS

EXPOSURE

Suit: _____

Undersuit _____

Gloves _____

Hood _____

Assessment: COLD OK HOT

DCI RISK

Was this dive...
- Cold Water Dive ☐
- Decompression Dive ☐
- Deep Dive ☐
- Excessive Work ☐
- Missed Deco. Stops ☐
- Rapid Ascent ☐

Are you...
- Dehydrated ☐

TIDES

HIGH WATER :

LOW WATER :

SLACK WATER :

CURRENT _____ kn   DIRECTION _____ °

SEA CONDITIONS

SEA STATE

WATER TEMP

VISIBILITY

BEAUFORT SCALE

EQUIPMENT

Notes on additional equipment ...

_____
_____
_____
_____

Skipper   **Boat**

Accumulated Dive Time To Date	Dive Time this Dive	Total Dive Time To Date
:	:	:

Verification Signature   **Certification No.**

Dive Record

Dive No | **Date**

Dive Site

AIR
START psi/bar − END psi/bar = psi/bar × CYLINDER CAPACITY = AIR USED

SURFACE AIR BREATHING RATE = ltr per min

TIME
SURFACE INTERVAL : | IN : > OUT : = DIVE DURATION × ABSOLUTE PRESSURE

DECO - DEPTH
DECOMPRESSION / SAFETY STOPS

____ mins at ____ m/ft ____ %

____ mins at ____ m/ft ____ %

____ mins at ____ m/ft ____ %

PRE DIVE GROUP | MAX DEPTH | END DIVE GROUP

Safety Margin: None 5% 10% 15% 20%

Computer / Decompression Tables Used:

WEIGHT

Weight Belt: ____ Kg/lbs

Integral BCD: ____ Kg/lbs

Ankle Weights: ____ Kg/lbs

Buoyancy: NEG - OK - POS

EXPOSURE

Suit: ____

Undersuit ____

Gloves ____

Hood ____

Assessment: COLD OK HOT

DCI RISK

Was this dive...
- Cold Water Dive ☐
- Decompression Dive ☐
- Deep Dive ☐
- Excessive Work ☐
- Missed Deco. Stops ☐
- Rapid Ascent ☐

Are you...
- Dehydrated ☐

TIDES

HIGH WATER :

LOW WATER :

SLACK WATER :

CURRENT ____ kn DIRECTION ____ °

SEA CONDITIONS

SEA STATE

WATER TEMP

VISIBILITY

BEAUFORT SCALE

EQUIPMENT

Notes on additional equipment ...

____

____

____

____

Skipper | **Boat**

Accumulated Dive	Dive Time	Total Dive
Time To Date	this Dive	Time To Date
:	:	:

Verification Signature　　　　　　　　Certification No.

Dive Record

Dive No | **Date**

Dive Site

AIR

START psi/bar − END psi/bar = psi/bar × CYLINDER CAPACITY = AIR USED

SURFACE AIR BREATHING RATE = ltr per min

TIME

SURFACE INTERVAL : | IN : > OUT : = DIVE DURATION × ABSOLUTE PRESSURE

DECO - DEPTH

DECOMPRESSION / SAFETY STOPS

_____ mins at _____ m/ft _____ %

_____ mins at _____ m/ft _____ %

_____ mins at _____ m/ft _____ %

PRE DIVE GROUP | MAX DEPTH | END DIVE GROUP

Safety Margin: None 5% 10% 15% 20%

Computer / Decompression Tables Used:

WEIGHT

Weight Belt:_____ Kg/lbs

Integral BCD:_____ Kg/lbs

Ankle Weights:_____ Kg/lbs

Buoyancy: NEG - OK - POS

EXPOSURE

Suit:_____

Undersuit_____

Gloves_____

Hood_____

Assessment: COLD OK HOT

DCI RISK

Was this dive...
Cold Water Dive ☐
Decompression Dive ☐
Deep Dive ☐
Excessive Work ☐
Missed Deco. Stops ☐
Rapid Ascent ☐
Are you...
Dehydrated ☐

TIDES

HIGH WATER :

LOW WATER :

SLACK WATER :

CURRENT _____ kn   DIRECTION _____ °

SEA CONDITIONS

SEA STATE

WATER TEMP

VISIBILITY

BEAUFORT SCALE

EQUIPMENT

Notes on additional equipment ...

Skipper | **Boat**

Accumulated Dive Time To Date	Dive Time this Dive	Total Dive Time To Date
:	:	:

Verification Signature   **Certification No.**

Dive Record

Dive No | **Date**

Dive Site

AIR
START psi/bar − END psi/bar = psi/bar × CYLINDER CAPACITY = AIR USED

SURFACE AIR BREATHING RATE = ltr per min

TIME
SURFACE INTERVAL : | IN : > OUT : = DIVE DURATION × ABSOLUTE PRESSURE

DECO - DEPTH
DECOMPRESSION / SAFETY STOPS

_____ mins at _____ m/ft _____ %

_____ mins at _____ m/ft _____ %

_____ mins at _____ m/ft _____ %

PRE DIVE GROUP | MAX DEPTH | END DIVE GROUP

Safety Margin: None 5% 10% 15% 20%

Computer / Decompression Tables Used:

WEIGHT

Weight Belt: _____ Kg/lbs

Integral BCD: _____ Kg/lbs

Ankle Weights: _____ Kg/lbs

Buoyancy: NEG - OK - POS

EXPOSURE

Suit: _____

Undersuit _____

Gloves _____

Hood _____

Assessment: COLD OK HOT

DCI RISK

Was this dive...
Cold Water Dive ☐
Decompression Dive ☐
Deep Dive ☐
Excessive Work ☐
Missed Deco. Stops ☐
Rapid Ascent ☐
Are you...
Dehydrated ☐

TIDES

HIGH WATER :

LOW WATER :

SLACK WATER :

CURRENT _____ kn   DIRECTION _____ °

SEA CONDITIONS

SEA STATE

WATER TEMP

VISIBILITY

BEAUFORT SCALE

EQUIPMENT

Notes on additional equipment ...

_____

_____

_____

_____

Skipper | Boat

Accumulated Dive Time To Date	Dive Time this Dive	Total Dive Time To Date
:	:	:

Verification Signature   Certification No.

Dive Record

Dive No

Date

Dive Site

AIR

| START psi/bar | − | END psi/bar | = | psi/bar | × | CYLINDER CAPACITY | = | AIR USED |

SURFACE AIR BREATHING RATE = _____ ltr per min

TIME

| SURFACE INTERVAL : | | IN : | > | OUT : | = | DIVE DURATION | × | ABSOLUTE PRESSURE |

DECO - DEPTH

DECOMPRESSION / SAFETY STOPS

_____ mins at _____ m/ft _____ %

_____ mins at _____ m/ft _____ %

_____ mins at _____ m/ft _____ %

PRE DIVE GROUP

MAX DEPTH

END DIVE GROUP

Safety Margin: None 5% 10% 15% 20%

Computer / Decompression Tables Used:

WEIGHT

Weight Belt: _____ Kg/lbs

Integral BCD: _____ Kg/lbs

Ankle Weights: _____ Kg/lbs

Buoyancy: NEG - OK - POS

EXPOSURE

Suit: _____

Undersuit _____

Gloves _____

Hood _____

Assessment: COLD OK HOT

DCI RISK

Was this dive...
- Cold Water Dive ☐
- Decompression Dive ☐
- Deep Dive ☐
- Excessive Work ☐
- Missed Deco. Stops ☐
- Rapid Ascent ☐

Are you...
- Dehydrated ☐

TIDES

HIGH WATER	:
LOW WATER	:
SLACK WATER	:

CURRENT _____ kn   DIRECTION _____ °

SEA CONDITIONS

SEA STATE

WATER TEMP

VISIBILITY

BEAUFORT SCALE

EQUIPMENT

Notes on additional equipment ...

_____

_____

_____

_____

_____

Skipper   **Boat**

Accumulated Dive Time To Date	Dive Time this Dive	Total Dive Time To Date
:	:	:

Verification Signature   Certification No.

Dive Record

Dive No **Date**

Dive Site

AIR
| START psi/bar | − | END psi/bar | = | psi/bar | × | CYLINDER CAPACITY | = | AIR USED |

SURFACE AIR BREATHING RATE
_____ ltr per min

TIME
| SURFACE INTERVAL : | IN : | > | OUT : | = | DIVE DURATION | × | ABSOLUTE PRESSURE |

DECO - DEPTH

DECOMPRESSION / SAFETY STOPS
_____ mins at _____ m/ft _____ %
_____ mins at _____ m/ft _____ %
_____ mins at _____ m/ft _____ %

PRE DIVE GROUP   **MAX DEPTH**   **END DIVE GROUP**

Safety Margin: None 5% 10% 15% 20%

Computer / Decompression Tables Used:

WEIGHT

Weight Belt: _____ Kg/lbs

Integral BCD: _____ Kg/lbs

Ankle Weights: _____ Kg/lbs

Buoyancy: NEG - OK - POS

EXPOSURE

Suit: _____
Undersuit _____
Gloves _____
Hood _____
Assessment: COLD OK HOT

DCI RISK

Was this dive...
Cold Water Dive ☐
Decompression Dive ☐
Deep Dive ☐
Excessive Work ☐
Missed Deco. Stops ☐
Rapid Ascent ☐
Are you...
Dehydrated ☐

TIDES

HIGH WATER :

LOW WATER :

SLACK WATER :

CURRENT _____ kn   DIRECTION _____ °

SEA CONDITIONS

SEA STATE

WATER TEMP

VISIBILITY

BEAUFORT SCALE

EQUIPMENT

Notes on additional equipment ...

Skipper   **Boat**

Accumulated Dive Time To Date	Dive Time this Dive	Total Dive Time To Date
:	:	:

Verification Signature　　　　　　**Certification No.**

Dive Record

Dive No | **Date**

Dive Site

AIR

START psi/bar − END psi/bar = psi/bar × CYLINDER CAPACITY = AIR USED

SURFACE AIR BREATHING RATE = ltr per min

TIME

SURFACE INTERVAL : | IN : > OUT : = DIVE DURATION × ABSOLUTE PRESSURE

DECO - DEPTH

DECOMPRESSION / SAFETY STOPS

_____ mins at _____ m/ft _____ %
_____ mins at _____ m/ft _____ %
_____ mins at _____ m/ft _____ %

PRE DIVE GROUP | MAX DEPTH | END DIVE GROUP

Safety Margin: None 5% 10% 15% 20%

Computer / Decompression Tables Used:

WEIGHT

Weight Belt: _____ Kg/lbs

Integral BCD: _____ Kg/lbs

Ankle Weights: _____ Kg/lbs

Buoyancy: NEG - OK - POS

EXPOSURE

Suit: _____
Undersuit _____
Gloves _____
Hood _____
Assessment: COLD OK HOT

DCI RISK

Was this dive...
Cold Water Dive ☐
Decompression Dive ☐
Deep Dive ☐
Excessive Work ☐
Missed Deco. Stops ☐
Rapid Ascent ☐
Are you...
Dehydrated ☐

TIDES

HIGH WATER :

LOW WATER :

SLACK WATER :

CURRENT _____ kn | DIRECTION _____ °

SEA CONDITIONS

SEA STATE

WATER TEMP

VISIBILITY

BEAUFORT SCALE

EQUIPMENT

Notes on additional equipment ...

Skipper | Boat

Accumulated Dive Time To Date	Dive Time this Dive	Total Dive Time To Date
:	:	:

Verification Signature   Certification No.

Dive Record

Dive No | **Date**

Dive Site

AIR: START psi/bar − END psi/bar = psi/bar × CYLINDER CAPACITY = AIR USED

SURFACE AIR BREATHING RATE = ltr per min

TIME: SURFACE INTERVAL : | IN : | OUT : | DIVE DURATION = | × ABSOLUTE PRESSURE

DECO - DEPTH:

DECOMPRESSION / SAFETY STOPS
_____ mins at _____ m/ft _____ %
_____ mins at _____ m/ft _____ %
_____ mins at _____ m/ft _____ %

PRE DIVE GROUP | MAX DEPTH | END DIVE GROUP

Safety Margin: None 5% 10% 15% 20%

Computer / Decompression Tables Used:

WEIGHT

Weight Belt: _____ Kg/lbs

Integral BCD: _____ Kg/lbs

Ankle Weights: _____ Kg/lbs

Buoyancy: NEG - OK - POS

EXPOSURE

Suit: _____

Undersuit _____

Gloves _____

Hood _____

Assessment: COLD OK HOT

DCI RISK

Was this dive...
Cold Water Dive ☐
Decompression Dive ☐
Deep Dive ☐
Excessive Work ☐
Missed Deco. Stops ☐
Rapid Ascent ☐
Are you...
Dehydrated ☐

TIDES

HIGH WATER :

LOW WATER :

SLACK WATER :

CURRENT _____ kn   DIRECTION _____ °

SEA CONDITIONS

SEA STATE

WATER TEMP

VISIBILITY

BEAUFORT SCALE

EQUIPMENT

Notes on additional equipment ...

Skipper | **Boat**

Accumulated Dive Time To Date	Dive Time this Dive	Total Dive Time To Date
:	:	:

Verification Signature　　　　　　　　Certification No.

Dive Record

Dive No | Date

Dive Site

AIR
START psi/bar − END psi/bar = psi/bar × CYLINDER CAPACITY = AIR USED
SURFACE AIR BREATHING RATE = ltr per min

TIME
SURFACE INTERVAL : | IN : > OUT : = DIVE DURATION × ABSOLUTE PRESSURE

DECO - DEPTH
DECOMPRESSION / SAFETY STOPS
____mins at ____m/ft ____%
____mins at ____m/ft ____%
____mins at ____m/ft ____%

PRE DIVE GROUP | MAX DEPTH | END DIVE GROUP

Safety Margin: None 5% 10% 15% 20%

Computer / Decompression Tables Used:

WEIGHT

Weight Belt:_____Kg/lbs

Integral BCD:_____Kg/lbs

Ankle Weights:_____Kg/lbs

Buoyancy: NEG - OK - POS

EXPOSURE

Suit:_____

Undersuit_____

Gloves_____

Hood_____

Assessment: COLD OK HOT

DCI RISK

Was this dive...
Cold Water Dive ☐
Decompression Dive ☐
Deep Dive ☐
Excessive Work ☐
Missed Deco. Stops ☐
Rapid Ascent ☐
Are you...
Dehydrated ☐

TIDES

HIGH WATER :

LOW WATER :

SLACK WATER :

CURRENT DIRECTION
____kn ____°

SEA CONDITIONS

SEA STATE

WATER TEMP

VISIBILITY

BEAUFORT SCALE

EQUIPMENT

Notes on additional equipment ...
_____
_____
_____
_____
_____

Skipper   Boat

Accumulated Dive Time To Date	Dive Time this Dive	Total Dive Time To Date
:	:	:

Verification Signature Certification No.

Dive Record

Dive No | **Date**

Dive Site

AIR
- START psi/bar − END psi/bar = psi/bar × CYLINDER CAPACITY = AIR USED
- SURFACE AIR BREATHING RATE = ltr per min

TIME
- SURFACE INTERVAL :
- IN :
- OUT :
- DIVE DURATION =
- ABSOLUTE PRESSURE ×

DECO - DEPTH
DECOMPRESSION / SAFETY STOPS
- _____ mins at _____ m/ft _____ %
- _____ mins at _____ m/ft _____ %
- _____ mins at _____ m/ft _____ %

PRE DIVE GROUP | MAX DEPTH | END DIVE GROUP

Safety Margin: None 5% 10% 15% 20%

Computer / Decompression Tables Used:

WEIGHT
Weight Belt: _____ Kg/lbs
Integral BCD: _____ Kg/lbs
Ankle Weights: _____ Kg/lbs
Buoyancy: NEG - OK - POS

EXPOSURE
Suit: _____
Undersuit _____
Gloves _____
Hood _____
Assessment: COLD OK HOT

DCI RISK
Was this dive...
- Cold Water Dive ☐
- Decompression Dive ☐
- Deep Dive ☐
- Excessive Work ☐
- Missed Deco. Stops ☐
- Rapid Ascent ☐

Are you...
- Dehydrated ☐

TIDES
- HIGH WATER :
- LOW WATER :
- SLACK WATER :
- CURRENT _____ kn DIRECTION _____ °

SEA CONDITIONS
- SEA STATE
- WATER TEMP
- VISIBILITY
- BEAUFORT SCALE

EQUIPMENT
Notes on additional equipment ...

Skipper | **Boat**

| Accumulated Dive Time To Date | Dive Time this Dive | Total Dive Time To Date |

: : :

Verification Signature   Certification No.

Dive Record

Dive No | Date

Dive Site

AIR

| START psi/bar | − | END psi/bar | = | psi/bar | × | CYLINDER CAPACITY | = | AIR USED |

SURFACE AIR BREATHING RATE = ltr per min

TIME

SURFACE INTERVAL : | IN : | > | OUT : | = | DIVE DURATION | × | ABSOLUTE PRESSURE

DECO - DEPTH

DECOMPRESSION / SAFETY STOPS

_____ mins at _____ m/ft _____ %

_____ mins at _____ m/ft _____ %

_____ mins at _____ m/ft _____ %

PRE DIVE GROUP | MAX DEPTH | END DIVE GROUP

Safety Margin: None 5% 10% 15% 20%

Computer / Decompression Tables Used:

WEIGHT

Weight Belt: _____ Kg/lbs

Integral BCD: _____ Kg/lbs

Ankle Weights: _____ Kg/lbs

Buoyancy: NEG - OK - POS

EXPOSURE

Suit: _____

Undersuit _____

Gloves _____

Hood _____

Assessment: COLD OK HOT

DCI RISK

Was this dive...
Cold Water Dive ☐
Decompression Dive ☐
Deep Dive ☐
Excessive Work ☐
Missed Deco. Stops ☐
Rapid Ascent ☐
Are you...
Dehydrated ☐

TIDES

HIGH WATER :

LOW WATER :

SLACK WATER :

CURRENT _____ kn   DIRECTION _____ °

SEA CONDITIONS

SEA STATE

WATER TEMP

VISIBILITY

BEAUFORT SCALE

EQUIPMENT

Notes on additional equipment ...

Skipper | Boat

Accumulated Dive Time To Date	Dive Time this Dive	Total Dive Time To Date
:	:	:

Verification Signature   Certification No.

Dive Record

Dive No | Date

Dive Site

AIR: START psi/bar − END psi/bar = psi/bar × CYLINDER CAPACITY = AIR USED / ABSOLUTE PRESSURE = SURFACE AIR BREATHING RATE ltr per min

TIME: SURFACE INTERVAL : | IN : > OUT : = DIVE DURATION × ABSOLUTE PRESSURE

DECO - DEPTH:
DECOMPRESSION / SAFETY STOPS
____ mins at ____ m/ft ____ %
____ mins at ____ m/ft ____ %
____ mins at ____ m/ft ____ %

PRE DIVE GROUP | MAX DEPTH | END DIVE GROUP

Safety Margin: None 5% 10% 15% 20%

Computer / Decompression Tables Used:

WEIGHT

Weight Belt: _____ Kg/lbs

Integral BCD: _____ Kg/lbs

Ankle Weights: _____ Kg/lbs

Buoyancy: NEG - OK - POS

EXPOSURE

Suit: _____
Undersuit _____
Gloves _____
Hood _____
Assessment: COLD OK HOT

DCI RISK

Was this dive...
Cold Water Dive ☐
Decompression Dive ☐
Deep Dive ☐
Excessive Work ☐
Missed Deco. Stops ☐
Rapid Ascent ☐
Are you...
Dehydrated ☐

TIDES

HIGH WATER :

LOW WATER :

SLACK WATER :

CURRENT ____ kn   DIRECTION ____ °

SEA CONDITIONS

SEA STATE

WATER TEMP

VISIBILITY

BEAUFORT SCALE

EQUIPMENT

Notes on additional equipment ...

Skipper | Boat

Accumulated Dive Time To Date	Dive Time this Dive	Total Dive Time To Date
:	:	:

Verification Signature Certification No.

Dive Record

Dive No | Date

Dive Site

AIR
START psi/bar − END psi/bar = psi/bar × CYLINDER CAPACITY = AIR USED

SURFACE AIR BREATHING RATE = ltr per min

TIME
SURFACE INTERVAL : | IN : > OUT : = DIVE DURATION × ABSOLUTE PRESSURE

DECO - DEPTH
DECOMPRESSION / SAFETY STOPS

_____ mins at _____ m/ft _____ %

_____ mins at _____ m/ft _____ %

_____ mins at _____ m/ft _____ %

PRE DIVE GROUP | MAX DEPTH | END DIVE GROUP

Safety Margin: None 5% 10% 15% 20%

Computer / Decompression Tables Used:

WEIGHT

Weight Belt: _____ Kg/lbs

Integral BCD: _____ Kg/lbs

Ankle Weights: _____ Kg/lbs

Buoyancy: NEG - OK - POS

EXPOSURE

Suit: _____

Undersuit _____

Gloves _____

Hood _____

Assessment: COLD   OK   HOT

DCI RISK

Was this dive...
Cold Water Dive ☐
Decompression Dive ☐
Deep Dive ☐
Excessive Work ☐
Missed Deco. Stops ☐
Rapid Ascent ☐
Are you...
Dehydrated ☐

TIDES

HIGH WATER :

LOW WATER :

SLACK WATER :

CURRENT _____ kn   DIRECTION _____ °

SEA CONDITIONS

SEA STATE

WATER TEMP

VISIBILITY

BEAUFORT SCALE

EQUIPMENT

Notes on additional equipment ...

Skipper | Boat

Accumulated Dive Time To Date	Dive Time this Dive	Total Dive Time To Date
:	:	:

Verification Signature   **Certification No.**

Dive Record

Dive No | **Date**

Dive Site

AIR
START psi/bar − END psi/bar = psi/bar × CYLINDER CAPACITY = AIR USED / SURFACE AIR BREATHING RATE = ltr per min

TIME
SURFACE INTERVAL : | IN : > OUT : = DIVE DURATION × ABSOLUTE PRESSURE

DECO - DEPTH
DECOMPRESSION / SAFETY STOPS
____ mins at ____ m/ft ____ %
____ mins at ____ m/ft ____ %
____ mins at ____ m/ft ____ %

PRE DIVE GROUP | MAX DEPTH | END DIVE GROUP

Safety Margin: None 5% 10% 15% 20%

Computer / Decompression Tables Used:

WEIGHT

Weight Belt: ____ Kg/lbs

Integral BCD: ____ Kg/lbs

Ankle Weights: ____ Kg/lbs

Buoyancy: NEG - OK - POS

EXPOSURE

Suit: ____
Undersuit ____
Gloves ____
Hood ____
Assessment: COLD OK HOT

DCI RISK

Was this dive...
Cold Water Dive ☐
Decompression Dive ☐
Deep Dive ☐
Excessive Work ☐
Missed Deco. Stops ☐
Rapid Ascent ☐
Are you...
Dehydrated ☐

TIDES

HIGH WATER :

LOW WATER :

SLACK WATER :

CURRENT ____ kn DIRECTION ____ °

SEA CONDITIONS

SEA STATE

WATER TEMP

VISIBILITY

BEAUFORT SCALE

EQUIPMENT

Notes on additional equipment ...

Skipper | **Boat**

Accumulated Dive Time To Date	Dive Time this Dive	Total Dive Time To Date
:	:	:

Verification Signature Certification No.

CONTACT

NOTES

CONTACT

NOTES

CONTACT

NOTES